The Million Dollar Listing Social Media

The Ultimate Social Media Marketing Guide for Real Estate Professionals!

Sebastian Acosta

CONTENTS

Contents

ACKNOWLEDGMENTS

To my Mom, Dad, Evan, Julian, Baby Adrian, uncles, aunts, cousins, Christine, Chris, JT, Coach Pat, Roberto, Delia, Adrian, Melissa, Milton, Ram, Herbert, Axel, Mike, Guillermo, Lina, Jens, Rosa, Anselmo, Carolina, Avenik, Hernan, Ricardo, JJ, Javier, Irving, Jose Luis, Manuel and all my colleagues at Engel & Volkers.

Thank you to all my teachers, friends and colleagues.

Thank you to everyone that ever did business with me as each one of you taught me great lessons.

Last but not least, thank you, the reader for exploring the lessons contained within this book. You truly deserve to be thanked.

FOREWORD

BY CHRIS MCLAUGHLIN

*- Owner of 4 Keller Williams Realty Offices in the Tampa,
FL area with 880 agents*
- His offices represent over $1.3 billion in closed volume
*- Bestselling Book Author of "Chris McLaughlin's Guide to
Smart Real Estate Investing"*

In 2008, I wrote the foreword for Sebastian's book: "Make Millions with Foreclosures and Short Sales." I was honored to do this because I have always had great respect for him as a savvy business owner and a cutting-edge entrepreneur. His book was very successful at the time because very few people knew how to properly navigate the fore closure and short sale arena and the market at the time was flooded with them. Now that foreclosures are for the most part, a thing of the past, he has moved on to a new generation of real estate marketing. In the past 5 years, I have seen how hard he has worked in the Social Media arena.

Sebastian has been able to develop his Instagram pages to over a million followers which he uses to capture clients, investors, partners while also interacting with them on a regular basis. This guarantees that he is always on the top of mind of his network when it comes to buying, investing, renting or selling properties. Sebastian has been a Top Producer at Engel & Volkers for several years in a row and also a very successful property flipper.

I can see him growing his business to another level because of his consistency and knowledge when it comes to keeping up with new technologies. This book teaches most of the techniques he has been using, so it is a valuable guide for anyone in the industry. I would highly recommend it for you to utilize in your business technologies. This book teaches most of the techniques he has been using, so it is a valuable guide for anyone in the industry.

DESCRIPTION; MY STORY

I have always been obsessed with my real estate business, marketing and social media. As result, I have managed to become a Top Producer in every company I have been with.

However, the path to be a successful real estate agent has not been the smoothest for me. When the real estate crisis hit the U.S. in 2007, I lost all my properties and all my money. At 30 years old, I had to go back and live with parents while I figured out what my next move was. While this took several years, I constantly educated myself with books and attended seminars to learn as much as I could.

As well as being a Luxury Residential and Commercial Real Estate agent, today I also run a real estate investing company and a social media network with over 1 million followers. A recent achievement of mine is that I have been able to buy and sell 250 homes between 2012 and 2017. My past book- Make Millions with Foreclosure and Short Sales, together with my marketing and sales skills, have helped me get into the door at speaking engagements across the country. This has also opened an avenue for me to meet investors in my field from various countries looking to embark on joint venture deals.

Times have changed. Since there has been a slowdown in the foreclosure market, I've had more time to sit down and put into perspective what I am doing right, specifically in terms of my marketing, specifically Social Media. Like most of my readers, I have had a Facebook page since the days. I opened my page in 2006 and it grew rapidly. The number of followers had me concerned because my page is always maxed out at 5000 friends; Facebook forced me to create new business pages. These pages grow organically and steadily. Funny thing is, our explosion into social media did not take off until the last couple of years.

I stumbled across what I believe is my favorite platform for real estate: Instagram (IG). One night, at a Miami Heat Basketball, I was looking around and noticed how two 15-year-olds were sitting in front of me and not paying any attention to the game. Instead, they just couldn't get their heads out of their phones. I knew right then and there; which platform would become the next big thing in marketing. And I was right.

I embarked on the next logical step which was to learn as much as I could about the psychology and networking behind this booming platform.

Instagram serves as the perfect medium to showcase properties as it is a photo app that allows you to showcase your listings, homes, future developments, videos of your listings etc.

With my personal page @sebastianacosta, I used to post regularly about my family, friends, travel and some of my hobbies. The page was growing very slowly, especially because I kept it private. I also started noticing that every time I posted something related to my real estate business, hobbies or motivational quotes, I would get fewer than 30% of my regular likes. It even happened with one of my biggest passions: saving animals.

Majority of my posts only attracted a few likes. Luckily, I soon came to realize that you have to separate pages into specific topics to care to different audiences. IG allows you to have up to 5 pages at the same time on one device but there is no limit to the number of pages you can create.

On March 2013, I started an animal rights movement page, as I was very bothered by the killing of almost 1000 dolphins every year in Taiji, Japan. I was very touched by this (after watching The Cove movie) but none of my closest friends seemed to care when I posted about animal rights on my personal page. I knew I had to come up with something that was out of the ordinary; something unique.

This page has now grown to be the one of the top pages for animal rights in the world. For example, every time I post a dog that needs to be adopted, it finds a new owner in just a matter of a few hours.

I also help raise awareness about environmental issues and raise money for special causes in a very short period of time.

Description; My Story

My charity work was recognized and got me a U.S. award for my company for Community Service in 2015.

One of my other passions is yoga and health, so I have a page called @ThePowerofTantra with almost half a million followers. It combines Yoga, relationships and inspirational quotes. I have over 3 Million engagement views every week.

Ok, now back to our original topic: Real Estate IG pages, with a combination of a few hundred thousand followers divided into several categories:

- @BuildingsoftheFuture – Futuristic architecture and cool buildings around the globe
- @RealEstateGlobal – Cool properties around the globe
- @UncensoredLuxury – Luxury Lifestyle & Modern Homes
- @RealEstateInvest – Real Estate Investing
- @HomesinMiami – Realtor Page for the Miami market
- @MiamiMansion – 2nd Realtor Page for the Miami Market

This book will help you get acquainted with social media marketing for business – especially for real estate professionals who are just rising up the ranks. My book discusses what social media is, the numerous possibilities apart from the typical personal networking, and what different platforms and tools are available for you to utilize. I hope you will gain valuable knowledge on how to take advantage of this innovation to promote your brand and boost your business over time.

When it comes to social media marketing, most people market online in the traditional way, by overloading their social media profiles with sales and promotions. This doesn't work well anymore, not in 2018 or years to come. The best marketing strategy focuses on building relationships with people, engaging and identifying with their problems, providing value and sharing stories.

I am always building more pages. The IG pages listed above are just some that have attracted many followers. Every time I see a need for a market, I start something new and utilize the existing pages to drive traffic to this new site. I learn something new every day but have noticed an increase in buyers and investors thanks to the pages. I have been able to establish strong alliances and partnerships because of the extended reach throughout all of our platforms.

I now have strong tentacles to expand my marketing efforts to buyers on every continent. Of course, I understand there are limitations. Most baby boomers still do not have Instagram and are just barely getting into Facebook and LinkedIn. If you even dare mention other popular platforms like Snapchat or Pinterest, most of them have no clue what you are talking about.

Most social media outlets are still in the baby stages, so whatever I tell you today will be outdated in a year, a few months or maybe even tomorrow. It is up to you to stay up to date with the current trends of the market.

One of the first lessons is to understand your client. Who is your target? What are their interests? What do they like? What do they want to see? Then, the answers to these questions will help you tailor your content and product to suit their needs and elicit the best response to your service.

Always be yourself in your online presence but think of yourself as a media outlet. You are now a form of press; a new generation blogger. Each one of your pages should convey a different message as it has a different audience.

In any page that has clients or on your business pages, please try to avoid subjects like Religion, Politics, Weapons, views on sexuality and especially the subject of abortion. Divisive topics should be avoided, and it is always best to not engage in these trends. Neutral is best. I do not expect you to master all the platforms. In fact, if you manage to become the best at just one of them, your success in terms of ROI of your time is bound to pay off.

Also, understand that most of these platforms will drive traffic to your personal site and/ or Facebook profile page. Make sure that these sites are very well developed and highly professional. I will touch on each and every one of these topics throughout the book.

IMPACT OF DIGITAL MARKETING ON REAL ESTATE

The effect of digital marketing on the traditional form of marketing has been nothing short of astounding, and for a good reason. The digital marketing sphere opens avenues that provide a potential client with the opportunity to experience a personal connection to a business or company, simply because they are constantly exposed to content from the business on a regular basis via online platforms.

Such occurrences attract potential clients and consumers to try out your service that they had zero knowledge of before. The advantages of digital marketing for a real estate business far outweigh any negatives. Any real estate professional understands how competitive the market space is. The onus is on you to secure that big break by using all the tools available to you in the digital marketing world to get your service to your preferred target audience.

Marketers are always looking for an edge – the best way to grow the reach of their business and acquire new customers without spending a lot of time or money. They plan creative campaigns, use attention-grabbing promotions, and are always on the lookout for the best way to make their message go further. In general, they're trying to find out how to take their efforts and grow them.

If you're looking for types of marketing strategies for small businesses or just methods to help you get the most out of your marketing efforts and advertising budget, here are a few suggestions.

Automation

One of the essential business marketing strategies is automation. Automation can mean many things, but one of the most important ways it is utilized is when it comes to amplifying your business marketing strategy through email. Email marketing automation is

beneficial when it comes to making sure your marketing strategy is more effective and helping your marketing convert to customers.

One way automating emails does this is through simple exposure. Setting up several emails to be sent to customers rather than just one means your customers will see your business name and product more. Even if that email doesn't convert them to a sale, it might mean still get you recall for your business.

Also, email automation is easy to tailor to your customer's journey. If your customer put an item into their online cart but didn't purchase, you can automate several emails that will remind the customer to complete their purchase, or even offer them a discounted price if they complete their investment in a certain amount of time.

Share and Share Again

Once you publish a blog or an ad, you don't just want to let it linger on the internet and hope that someone finds it.

You want to share it on your company's social pages or boost it so that it can be seen by more people on places like Facebook, Twitter, and Instagram. Even spending just a few dollars to promote a post or an ad can help you reach a bigger audience and that can make a big difference, depending on your goals.

You should also engage with your employees and ask them to share the content they find interesting and relevant. This not only helps grow your reach, but it makes your employees feel like they're a part of the big picture of your business goals.

Analytics and Testing

One of the best ways to amplify your business marketing strategy is to make sure you're not using a technique that doesn't work. Making sure that you're testing your emails and social posts and always watching your analytics to track results is key.

Analytics let you see the direct correlation between your digital marketing efforts and results, like web visitors. If something is taking a lot of time or money, but you never see any results from it, then you might cut that from your business marketing strategy ideas and executions list.

If you are only ever sending out one email or social media post, and never testing things like different images or different copy or different messaging, you might be missing out on an excellent opportunity to find the right mix of elements that resonate with your customers and drives action.

The Art of Implementing Marketing Automation for Your Brand

You have probably heard the term "marketing automation" constantly being thrown around in marketing circles. Think of it as software or tactic that exists with the purpose of automating repetitive tasks like social media, emails, and other website actions. Automating marketing actions makes these tasks easier.

A perfect example of marketing automation is Amazon – who uses marketing automation to nurture prospects with personalized content that eventually turns these leads into customers. Though it can be a tricky marketing initiative, marketing automation is not impossible to execute.

Let me paint a scenario for you: To grow a plant, you need feeble soil to aid the growth of the plant. The next step is to get seeds, and lastly, water and so light to nurture the seeds into becoming a blossoming plant. It isn't usually that easy, but it is not impossible. You can only for you have nurtured the leads (seedlings) into becoming a paying customer (lush, blossoming plant).

Learning how to execute integrated marketing automation for your brand is a vital aspect marketing strategy. I will be sharing tips that guarantee a successful implementation of marketing automation with digital marketing trends.

Marketing automation has been drifting away from its tag as a trend to becoming an essential marketing strategy tool. Studies show that up to 91% of marketing automation users think it is a crucial part of their overall marketing strategy. However, to successfully carry out marketing automation, it is smart to plan the process and carry out a robust implementation process as well.

If you are considering marketing automation as part of your brand's strategy, I have provided some tips that should help you during the process:

What Is the Point of Marketing Automation?

The first step involves learning what marketing automation is all about, it's key benefits and expected outcome when implemented. The primary purpose of marketing automation is to optimize. Instead of wasting time on repetitive tasks, modern technology is being used by businesses to increase productivity. Marketing automation possesses the potential to achieve maximum productivity and more.

Generate Stronger Leads: A tangible benefit of marketing automation tools is that it provides you with quick knowledge of how your consumers think; hereby creating better quality leads that can convert them. Inbound marketing represents a surefire way to attract real estate clients through leads that can elevate your strategy to a new level.

For example, some email marketing automation platforms allow you to analyze which newsletters your consumers expressed interest in the most, and you can use such tools to choose the best properties to offer your clients. This will improve the quality of your leads because you now have a better understanding of your consumers' train of thought in the sales funnel.

Cut Back On Marketing Costs: Marketing automation solutions can carry out multiple tasks, which reduces the costs associated with a massive marketing team. You can save money with a smaller marketing team and invest the money elsewhere. By lowering costs, your business can invest in more properties and grow.

Increases Revenue: Businesses are run for the sole purpose of making profit, and a met benefit of marketing automation is to triple your revenue. Real estate firms that use automated lead engagement software experienced a 10% increase in their income over a 56-month period, according to a Gartner research.

With marketing automation, you can grow your revenue and cut costs, and I would sign up for such an excellent marketing tactic immediately

Implementing Marketing Automation for Brand

Have you decided to try out marketing automation? Then, you need to learn how to apply this marketing strategy to your business. The steps highlighted below will help you successfully implement marketing automation:

- Set Your Goals: Despite its numerous benefits, marketing automation costs money and time to implement, which means that you need to properly analyze your business strategy to understand if marketing automation is beneficial to real estate and specifically, the type of business you operate. Once you've decided that marketing automation is a strategy you would like to implement into your business, you can now move on to the next steps: Do you want to expand your clientele? As a Real estate professional, do you need to optimize your marketing process to generate better leads? Understand what you wish to accomplish with a marketing automation strategy.

- Have A Plan: Like other marketing strategies, it is critical for a real estate professional to have a plan. A lot of technical jargons that you will have to deal with during the implementation process include adhering customer data, defining your KPIs, and learning how to integrate automation into your marketing strategy. Because of the complex manner of marketing automation, it is very important to plan the process accordingly.

- Choose the appropriate Marketing Automation Solution: After creating a plan and setting your goal and budget, it is finally time to pick a marketing automation software solution to use. To help you narrow down the best solution, use the following criteria: Integration compatibility, pricing, user-friendliness, and features. The solution that passes all the tests should perfectly suit your real estate business model.

Marketing automation solutions provide positive results if your company implements the process correctly. The key is choosing the perfect platform which will guarantee a smooth implementation. Take these tips under advisement and you can rest assured of success.

CHAPTER ONE:
YOUR WEBSITE

Before getting into the nuts and bolts of social networking, I want to talk briefly about your website. Everything in this book assumes that you have a website. If you don't already have a website, get one as soon as possible. In case your existing real estate company doesn't give you a page, the easiest and cheapest way to create one is by to out sourcing the job to freelancers.

They will competitively bid on the project to design your website. You can do this by utilizing freelancing platforms such as freelancer.com, Upwork, Craigslist, Guru, 99designs, Peopleperhour, etc. and post a new project for a website.

The project is the design of your website. Thousands of freelance web designers from all over the world will bid on your project. After receiving as many bids as you require, review the portfolio of the websites that these individuals have completed. Choose someone whose work impresses you, who has completed a lot of prior jobs and has many favorable online reviews. This will be a lot cheaper than calling up a local web developer. Usually the turnaround time will be quick, and the website will often look better. It should not cost more than $1000 to get a really good and professional looking website. Many freelancers can create a nice website for half that amount. I suggest creating your website as a WordPress Blog; having your website in a blog format will allow you to constantly add content to it.

Everything you read in this book might end up being useless if you don't have a website. The majority of strategies in this book specifically outline how to bring more leads to your website. So, I assume that you have a professional website. If you are unsure if your website looks good, then simply go to Google and type in your profession and city. For example, if you are a Realtor® and you live in Miami, type "Realtor Miami" into Google and see what shows up in the search results.

Click on the first twenty realtor websites that show up in the search results. Make a list of the 3 websites you think are most professional. That is probably how you want your web site to look. If you do this exercise, you will notice two things. You will instantly see that the first few listings that come up are from extremely web savvy companies. These companies know how to market by using the internet. These websites are designed well, packed with information and look very professional.

The second thing you will notice is, by scrolling through the majority of the search results on the first few pages, you'll discover that the vast majority of these websites look very boring and plain.

Many websites consist of a banner at the top with five to seven tabs and a menu on the left or right. Do not make a website with this design unless you like to be boring. Your website should stand out. The reason many sites look like this is because they are designed using templates. It is better to custom design a web site by hiring a freelancer on freelancer.com, Upwork, Craigslist, Guru, 99designs, Peopleperhour, among other freelance sites.

You only get one chance to make a good first impression. If you meet someone at a business meeting or networking event, give them your business card. There is a good chance they will check out your website if it's listed on your card.

Everything in this book will teach you strategies and methods to drive traffic and leads to your website. You need to make sure that when people get to your website, they do not immediately leave. Your site needs to be packed with information so that they stay and visit it again. If the website looks unprofessional, then you have ruined your chance to make a great first impression.

Chapter One: Your Website

The same concept applies to your business card, logo and overall image. Don't skimp on these things. Pay more to get a professional looking business card. Apply the same concept to your website.

I would recommend having a colored picture on your business card as this will help people remember you. Also, leave some white space on the card to allow people to take notes. Do the same with your logo so that you stand out from everyone else.

Marketing experts say that it takes 5 to 7 "touches" for consumers to be ready to do business with you. When you meet someone at a meeting, consider that **touch**:

1. When they start chatting with you and take your business card
2. If they visit your website
3. If you connect with them online on a site like Facebook or LinkedIn
4. If you meet them again and have a meaningful conversation with them

At that point, if they like you, they will most likely begin to ask others about you. They will want to know if you are a person worthy of doing business with them and their referrals. They will also want to know if you can refer business to them. Most people don't complete all of the above steps and never get this far. I cannot tell you how many people I meet every month at real estate meetings that don't even have a business card.

And if you manage to get this far, please make sure to be an expert in your field. No one wants to refer business to someone that does not know what they're doing. If you are not an expert in your field, either change fields or spend more time studying your profession to become one! A book I recommend is Outliers by Malcom Gladwell, which explains the key elements that define successful people.

In this book, there is a chapter about branding which explains the concept of branding in detail. Branding is very important as it is the image you are projecting to the world. Think about your brand before you design your business card, logo and website.

In summary, with regards to websites, it is important to have a good, professional looking one. Spend the money necessary to make it look good. Now if you start generating leads with the strategies you learn in this book, you won't scare your visitors away.

Remember that all of the techniques in this book focus on driving traffic and leads to your website. I cannot emphasize enough how important this is. Make sure you do this before you start applying all of the social networking and internet marketing tips in this book.

CHAPTER TWO:
SOCIAL NETWORKING

A Social Network is an online community of people who share interests and/or activities. Most social networking sites are web based and provide a variety of ways for users to interact, such as allowing users to email and instant message other users.

The following table lists the 15 most popular social networking websites ranked by a combination of inbound links, Alexa rank, and U.S traffic data from Compete and Quantcast. This list was compiled in January 2017.

15 Most Popular Social Networking Websites

1. Facebook
2. YouTube
3. Instagram
4. Twitter
5. Reddit
6. Vine (In January 2017, Vine became the VineCamera)
7. Pinterest
8. Ask.fm
9. Tumblr
10. Flickr
11. Google+
12. LinkedIn
13. VK

14. Classmates

15. Meetup

Social networking sites are used regularly by millions of people. Popular ones in the United States include Facebook, Twitter, LinkedIn and Meetup. These four dominate social networking with their amount of online traffic. There are hundreds of other social networking sites with many newer ones being developed every month. Some social networking sites are more popular in other countries than they are in the U.S. Many people have never heard of half of the websites on the above list.

Facebook alone has over 1 billion users and 750 million unique monthly visitors. Twitter has 250 million unique monthly visitors, LinkedIn has 110 million and Meetup has more than 70 million.

This means that just the top four social networking sites have a combined total of almost 1.2 billion unique monthly visitors! Considering that there are only 7 billion people on the planet, which is a tremendous amount of web traffic. All of that web traffic could generate a lot of potential leads, leads which could be coming to your website. So, the next time you hear someone say, "Why do I need to be on Facebook?" tell them, "You cannot afford not to be on Facebook."

Keep in mind, the above list is not ranking the most visited websites but only the most visited social networking sites.

Here is a list of the 15 most popular websites compiled by Alexa, which ranks website traffic. For more info about Alexa visit their website: www.alexa.com. This list was compiled in January 2017.

15 Most Popular Web Sites in the World

1. Google.com

2. Youtube.com

3. Facebook.com

4. Baidu.com

5. Wikipedia.org

6. Yahoo.com

7. Reddit.com

8. Google.co.in

9. Qq.com

10. Twitter.com

11. Taobao.com

12. Amazon.com

13. Google.co.jp

14. Sohu.com

15. Tmall.com

In this list, the only social networking sites that are listed are Facebook, Twitter and Linked-In. Facebook has 7 times more monthly traffic than Linked-In and 3 times more monthly traffic than Twitter. Many business professionals have Linked-In profiles but have not yet registered on Facebook. You cannot afford to NOT be registered on Facebook. Facebook is simply the most popular social networking site on the planet.

These are the most visited websites with the highest traffic. You should think about how you and your business are listed on Google, Facebook, Yahoo, You Tube, MSN, Amazon, eBay and Twitter. Is your business on Bing? Do you advertise on Craigslist? Do you have a WordPress Blog? The traffic statistics in the above tables indicate that these are the most important websites in the world. If you want your business to grow and more customers, then you have to feature prominently online on these sites.

This is the new Yellow Pages. Throw your phone book away. Instead, put your business online and figure out how to get more exposure for your business using the above 15 sites. These sites have the traffic, which can be converted into leads that generate revenue. What you need to learn is how to get those leads and turn them into revenue.

Chapter Two: Social Networking

This book will address social networking sites in more detail. I'll explain how many of these sites operate and how they can help you market yourself and your business. One of the sites on the list is called Meetup.com, which is really a synthesis between an online site and an offline networking meeting place (hence the name meetup). Check the chapter below that covers www.meetup.comin more detail.

It is also important to distinguish the differences between social networking and internet marketing. Even though the two go hand-in-hand, there are some differences. Social networking involves becoming friends online with different people in a common forum like Facebook, Twitter or Linked-In. Internet marketing involves driving traffic to your website. This traffic generates leads which can turn into revenue. Traffic can come from another website or from offline methods such as signs, banners, postcards, flyers, etc. You can also drive traffic to your website from social networking sites. The reason this is so powerful is because it is free.

Finally, the last way to drive traffic to your web site is from search engines like Google, Yahoo and Bing. This traffic can come from organic searches, where your site shows up in the search results, or from paid advertising, which is called Pay per Click or PPC for short.

You can also drive traffic to your website from videos on You Tube, comments on Facebook, Tweets on Twitter, articles on your blog, Audio Podcasts, Lead Capture Pages, etc. There are literally hundreds of ways to drive traffic to your website. Social networking is only one of these ways. However, as you will see in this book, all of these topics are interrelated.

If you have a website with YouTube videos, capture pages, links to your social networking profiles and blog articles, then your website will register new content frequently with the search engines.

If your website also has good content and uses relevant keywords to your business or product, then search engines will index your website better than others. All of these concepts are interrelated. They are all part of your toolbox of social networking and internet marketing.

Since our business is primarily in the United States, I'll focus mostly on the above-mentioned social networking sites that are in English and target U.S. audiences. Naturally, if your business or product targets a foreign audience, you would want to include those sites in your social networking and internet marketing. Many networkers try and join every social networking site possible. I think that joining just the top sites and working efficiently with these networks is much better than having scattered profiles all over the web. There is one advantage to having many profiles though. Since the advent of services like *www.hootsuite.com,* it is becoming easier to update multiple profiles on multiple sites. I'll talk about Hootsuite in a later chapter.

If you look on *www.alexa.com,* you can see the demographics for any website, which can tell you a lot about your target audience. Linked-In consists primarily of users that are 35 to 44 years old. Many users on Linked-In have completed graduate school. Users of this social networking site are well-educated and sophisticated. If your target market consists of people in this age group with this demographic, Linked-In is perfect for you. This is one of the reasons why LinkedIn is so popular with recruiters and employers looking to hire.

These types of demographics are very important to an internet marketer. Using Linked-In to market a new graduate school program would be a bad idea. Many of the users have already completed graduate school and are pursuing their professional career. It is very important to research and understand demographics and your target audience. Once you understand your target audience and the demographic of your target audience, it will be easier for you to understand who to market to. For example, in the real estate industry, the National Association of Realtors publishes an annual report called "Profile of Home Buyers and Sellers". You can find this report by visiting www.realtor.org.

This report shows the following demographics:

- 41% of home buyers are first time buyers
- The first-time home buyer average age was 30
- The average repeat home buyer was 47
- Median income of buyers was $74,900
- 94% of buyers aged 25 to 44 used the internet to search for their homes.

I think that the final statistic is the one to pay attention to. If home buyers are primarily between 30 and 47 years old, and 94% of buyers in this age group are searching by internet, what does that tell you? If you are a real estate agent or in the business of real estate, then you need to have a presence on the internet. Specifically, you need to have a presence on the sites where consumers are searching. In the case of real estate, these sites would be *www.realtor.com, www. zillow.com,* and *www.trulia.com.* Your marketing offers should also include social networking sites and internet marketing techniques to capture leads.

85% of Facebook users are between the ages of 13 to 44. Many users on Linked-In have attended college and the average age is 25 to 44. Twitter is used by an average age group of 25 to 44-year-olds who have attended some college and some graduate school. What can you learn from these demographics? Well for one, many of the users of social networking sites have attended college. Second, you can learn that most users of social networking sites are primarily in their twenties, thirties, and early forties. In fact, forty-five years seems to be the cutoff, when usage drops off, according to Alexa.

Most people that are older than 45 are not using social networking sites (or computers) as much as people in their twenties, thirties, and early forties. And this makes sense. The web browser for Windows was invented in 1993. This is when using the internet started to become more popular. Many older computer users became proficient at using a computer when they were in college. These users usually advanced their computer skills when they entered the job market.

When I was in college in the early 90s, we used to look up information for research on services like Prodigy and CompuServe using dial-up modems. This was before the internet was popular because the web browser had not yet been invented.

In those early days of the internet, computer skills acquired in college were then translated into the job market. Many employers were requiring minimum computer skill aptitude levels such as knowing how to type and use software programs like Microsoft Word, Outlook, Excel, PowerPoint, etc.

If you used a computer in college and again in your first few jobs after college, you are probably very proficient and comfortable using a computer in your daily life. These people use the computer much more frequently and are likely to be visiting social networking sites and surfing the internet. If you were over thirty when you decided to see what all the fuss was about computers, email, and the World Wide Web, etc., then you are probably not as comfortable using a computer.

Obviously, these are very broad generalizations. There are many users in their sixties and seventies that are very proficient with computers and there also many users in their twenties that are not. However, speaking generally based on Alexa data, if the web browser was invented in 1993 and you were born before 1963, you might fit into the group that is less comfortable with computers.

These findings are directly correlated to Alexa rankings which show a sharp drop off over age 45 for users of social networking sites. Compare that to the 48% of 18- 34-year-olds who check Facebook upon waking up. The interesting part is that 28% of those groups do so before even getting out of bed! For more interesting facts and statistics about Facebook, check out this link on the Digital Buzz Blog: *http://www.digitalbuzzblog.com/facebook-statistics*-stats-facts-2011/.

I think that many older users don't understand the point of spending hours on social networking sites like Facebook. Hopefully by the

33

time you complete this book, you will have more insight into why it is worthwhile to allocate some of your time to social networking.

The younger generation doesn't view spending time on social networking sites as a chore. Quite the contrary, they spend all of their spare time on these sites and view it as fun. Marketers that target this demographic are constantly thinking about how to get online and in front of this huge audience. You can even buy Facebook Ads directly on Facebook and target the exact demographic you are looking for.

Since my business is real estate, I will focus my social networking emphasis on Facebook, Twitter and LinkedIn, which serves an older demographic of 30 to 47-year-olds. I will also address my favorite app: Instagram, which is one of the main tools to reach the millennial buyer and has older, tech-oriented users.

Before going into details on each of these, it is important to understand how to effectively use a social network to maximize the benefits of social networking. Social networking should be used as a way for you to introduce yourself and your services to as many people as possible. Do this by introducing yourself and your services to all of your friends and to many people that your friends know. This is the concept of six degrees of separation.

The way to become friends with people that are outside your network, is through either face to face interaction when networking or targeted marketing. Face to face interaction means going to networking events that your friends go to, in order to meet people, they know. Targeted marketing involves establishing a relationship with people that are in the same business as you or share common interests. For example, I enjoy yoga and together with a friend formed a group called the "The Power of Tantra online on Facebook". Other users on Facebook that are interested in yoga might join the group.

This is an example of networking with people who share common interests. My friend and I did not form this group to generate business. This group was formed to find more friends that love yoga. However, it also allows us to meet more people. When a person

34

becomes friends with us on Facebook, they automatically see what we do. We don't need to tell them. That is why it is so important to understand that your business presence and personal presence is one in the same thing. If your friends only know you personally online and you have no online business presence, then you probably are not getting much business. You are missing out on one of the easiest networking opportunities that are right under your nose.

In order for people to do business with you, they need to know you. They won't know you if you are sitting at home watching TV. So, go out and start socializing and networking to meet more people. The yoga group is an example of online social networking turned into face to face networking.

Do not make the mistake of assuming that business networking events are the only kind of networking there is. To emphasize on this, I met one of my biggest clients after a yoga class. She works as an investment banker and has introduced me to her circle of clients. Any face to face interaction is networking and having a joined interest like a hobby is a great way to meet people. The best kind of networking is interacting socially outside of a business environment, where you and the other person can get to know each other better. And having a joined interest like a hobby is a great way to meet people.

Another way of establishing targeted marketing is to use a capture page, also known as a squeeze page, or landing page. With this method, a one-page website is used to bring people in with an offer for a free product like an audio CD or eBook. This targeted traffic becomes part of your database that you can send emails to using email marketing. When you send your marketing message or introduction letter via email, include an invitation to connect with them online.

This method can tremendously increase your online network of friends and let others in your industry know who you are and what you do. You can network these individuals and do joint venture marketing together. This will benefit both yourself and these individuals by offering an opportunity to expand your circle of friends. It is a good idea to add your social network links in your signature line at the end of your emails. Every time you send someone an email, it is an opportunity to connect with them online.

Social networking is more sophisticated than, "Do you want to be friends with me?" So many people erroneously assume that social networking is a waste of time. However, effectively using social networking as a medium can and does bring in millions of dollars of revenue for businesses.

Some examples:

Dell Computers announced that it generated more than $10 million in sales from its Twitter and Facebook accounts. This is an example of millions of dollars in revenue created via social networking. Fox Interactive recently completed a media study on social networks and internet marketing. This study showed that social-network- based advertisements offered a substantially higher return on investment compared to all other advertising campaigns including television advertising!

The bottom line: adding social networking and internet marketing to your marketing efforts will increase your overall performance dramatically. Consider allocating thirty minutes a day to social networking and online internet marketing. You can make thousands of dollars in revenue by adding social networking and internet marking to your marketing efforts.

CHAPTER THREE:
ESTABLISHING YOUR BRAND

B randing is a marketing term. Since this book is about social networking. Since this book is about social networking, I am going to keep the concept of branding really short and sweet. Branding is about establishing your brand name. Branding is very important because this is what you show the world, and what the world sees when they see you. The best marketers spend considerable time building their brand.

Before you begin your business model, think about your brand and how you would like to be identified. You might think of Coca Cola or McDonald's when I mention branding. But in reality, small business owners have identities that can also become their brand name.

Donald Trump is a brand. It is also Donald Trump's name. He is a classic example of shameless self-promotion because he branded his own name. When you brand a company name, it is called advertising! Branding really works. Donald Trump's name is synonymous with luxury, high-end real estate. This is what I mean by establishing a brand name.

The first thing to decide about branding, before you start marketing, is whether to brand your name or your business name. For example, if your name is Jack Smith and your company is called Miami Mansions, there is a choice to brand yourself as Jack Smith or as Miami Mansion. In this case, the company name would make more sense since you are identifying your company by its service.

However, the choice of how you want to present yourself to the general public entirely is up to you. If you have decided on the company name, then you would brand all of your online networking and social marketing accounts as well as

Print material, websites, email addresses, business cards, and advertising with your brand name.

Examples

- Logo: Miami Mansion Real Estate Experts
- Business card: Logo of MiamiMansion
- Letterhead and Envelopes: Logo of MiamiMansion
- Email address:jack@MiamiMansion.com
- Website:www.MiamiMansion.com
- Facebook:www.facebook.com/MiamiMansion
- Twitter:www.twitter.com/MiamiMansion
- LinkedIn:www.linkedin.com/MiamiMansion
- You Tube:www.youtube.com/MiamiMansion

These are good examples of branding. If anyone visits your website, finds you on a social network, or sees your business card, they will instantly know what you do. You are an expert in MIAMI MANSION's (bank owned properties) and other people will know because you told them.

Believe it or not, it is hard to figure out what some people do. In the above example, does it matter if this person is a realtor with Homes in Miami, Miami Mansions, or another smaller real estate company? Not really.

What matters is that we know they are experts in Miami Mansion real estate. That is what they want you to know. The reason this works is because they have branded themselves. You should do the same thing with your brand and business.

Too many times I meet real estate agents that tell me they specialize in something like short sales. But when I look at their card and website, I don't see anything related to short sales. I assume that these individuals are just getting into the short sale game. If they really specialized in short sales, they would brand themselves as such and at least have the words "short sale" on their card.

Chapter Three: Establishing Your Brand

If someone specializes in short sales but their business cards, web sites etc. do not promote this, they are missing the boat by a mile. They are giving up a classic opportunity to get more business.

Simply designing a logo and web site with the name "Short Sale Expert" will allow them to brand themselves. After establishing their brand name, it is easy to have the same username on all social networking sites. Remember, people will not know what you do unless you tell them. When I say tell them, I am referring to what is on your business card, logo and website. No one remembers what was said at a networking meeting a month ago. That is why it is a good idea to have a photo on your business card. A photo will make it easier for people to remember who you are.

Once you have identified your brand and created a logo, you can now create matching business cards, stationery, etc. You can also display the logo on your website, business card and business stationery, etc. Now, you have a name that you can identify yourself with. You can change your entire social networking sites user ID's to match this brand name.

At this point, you will need to establish an "elevator speech." An elevator speech is thirty seconds or less. It is an explanation of yourself or your company. When someone asks what you do, your answer must be short and sweet like the time it takes to ride an elevator.

Write a long and short form biography about yourself or your company and save it as a document on your computer. You should have a full-form, long and short-form bio, which is a written version of the elevator speech. Then, simply copy and paste the information from the document into the various social networking sites that you join. This gives the advantage of not having to type the info each time you join a new social networking site. Additionally, it ensures that your message is consistent and well thought out, as opposed to writing it on the spot. Follow these tips and there will be no confusion about who you are and what you do.

You will also be less likely to have spelling or grammatical mistakes. Your bio should tell people what you do, how long you have been doing it, and list any of your achievements. Write something that reflects upon you in the best way. If you need guidance, look at biographies of prominent individuals on their websites or the inside covers of their books. By looking at other biographies, you will get some good ideas on how to formulate your own.

Be consistent. Make sure others see your brand and business the way you want them to. Work on establishing a biography, logo, and business image, with a little time and effort you will have one. This also directly relates to focus. If you have two or three different professions, you will only be able to focus 1/3 or ½ of your time on each one. Pick one that you enjoy the most or is the most financially rewarding. Shut down the others and focus. You will be amazed at the power of focusing.

A great book called Power of Focus by Jack Canfield talks about this concept. Focus on one business and one brand and it is easier to make yourself identifiable to the general public. It is also easier for you to focus your time and energy in being good at one thing. The more specialized and focused your brand is, the better.

A good photo to use for all your profile photos is necessary when establishing your presence on social networking sites. I recommend hiring a good photographer to capture the best shot of your face and half of your torso. Just keep in mind that your photo is part of your image.

Take some consideration of how you would like yourself to appear to others before choosing a photo. Hiring a professional photographer can sometimes be expensive. Some photographers offer bulk deals, which is cheaper, if you invite them to your office and they take pictures for all the agents.

Key Tips to Remember:

- You must have a brand with a logo
- Have a picture of yourself on your card
- You must use this brand name everywhere
- Your brand must be the same everywhere
- Your website must identify your brand
- Your email address should identify your brand

If your business card does not have an email address and website listed, then you are simply not serious about getting new business. Most business communication is now happening online via email. People don't have the time for long phone conversations. Email is efficient and there is no voicemail phone tag to deal with. I personally do a lot of business correspondence by texting. My clients know that by emailing or texting, they will get an immediate response. Calling will not. You need to get online now or risk losing your business to others that are.

Choosing a professional email address is extremely important. Even big business owners make this mistake and it is so easy to rectify. The email address, *Jack1980@hotmail.com* is not as professional as *jack@MiamiMansion.com.* The first email does not brand you well. The second one does. I will specifically discuss email addresses in a later chapter. People should instantly recognize what you do by your brand name, logo, website address and email address. It costs $10 per year to get a web domain name with email forwarding and is very inexpensive to set up a website.

After giving thought to your brand name and marketing image, the next thing to think about is social networking. The next chapter will discuss social networking, starting with the largest and most popular social networking site, Facebook. This is the best way to undergo .

CHAPTER FOUR:
FACEBOOK

Building an Online Community with Facebook

Facebook is not only an advertising and publishing platform. Only promoting your business on Facebook by creating ads linked to your sales page is greatly underutilizing the platform. To become successful at building your Facebook presence, create an online community with your customers as the members. There are multiple ways to do this and many ways to measure a person's level of participation in your community.

As a real estate agent, you must understand that success doesn't just occur because of your ability to sell a property. The ability to convert prospects and generate leads through engaging marketing campaigns is more essential to achieving success in a competitive field such as real estate.

In earlier times, most realtors relied on networking around their city, posting information on the local bulletin board, and perhaps even taking it a step further by going door-to-door to hand out flyers. Nowadays, this marketing strategy yields a low return. Half The people at the mall are glued to their smartphones, and the other half are lounging by the porch waiting for their Amazon delivery to arrive.

So, how can a real estate agent secure new leads in an increasingly technological society? Facebook, of course!

A study conducted by Mediakix shows that the average person spends more than half an hour each day on Facebook, which gives you, the realtor, a golden opportunity to get your business and properties in their faces with killer Facebook ads.

AVERAGE DAILY TIME SPENT ON SOCIAL

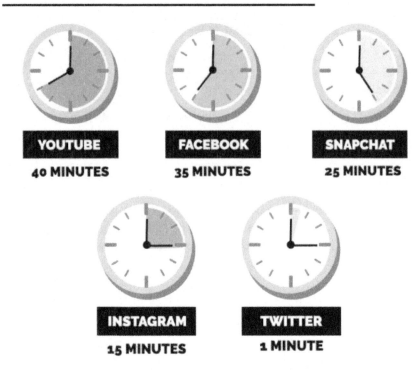

YOUTUBE	FACEBOOK	SNAPCHAT
40 MINUTES	**35 MINUTES**	**25 MINUTES**

INSTAGRAM	TWITTER
15 MINUTES	**1 MINUTE**

Facebook is all about liking what you see – just like real estate – and offers specified targeting options that allow you to reach your desired target audience , from wealthy coastal retirees to just-married home buyers.

Sure, Facebook advertising is the answer, but what is the marketing strategy behind Facebook ads? How can maximize your budget to make sure that you aren't wasting precious marketing spend on doomed campaigns?

Layer on Interests, Location, Demographic, and Behavioral Targeting Options

Facebook is the perfect platform to advertise your brand because of the specificity and detailed level of targeting available on the platform. After crafting the goal of the campaign, you can utilize the various targeting options to key on precise options, to be certain you're getting your ads to the correct audience.

1. Location Targeting by Zip Code

The first step is to set location targeting based on the area where you operate out of. It is important to not get overly precise – by targeting within a one-mile radius – as people continually move to and from other locations. Targeting zip codes that usually move to your base of operations based on precious selling history is a good way to start.

2. Targeting the Age Ranges

While this is self-explanatory, it is essential not to breeze over it. It isn't logical to show your ads to teenagers and expect them to buy a $2 million mansion you're attempting to sell.

3. Targeting by Income

Navigate **to *Detailed Targeting > Demographics > Financial > Income, you can reach out to a target audience based on their income. Awesome, right? This is a very valuable strategy that should be employed by any real estate agent since this process determines the type of property your leads can buy.*

Demographics > Financial > Income

4. $100,000 - $124,999

5. $125,000 - $149,999

6. $150,000 - $249,999

Demographics > Home > Home Ownership

First time homebuyer

Add demographics, interests or behaviors | **Suggestions** | Browse

▼ Income

1. $40,000 - $49,999 ☐

2. $50,000 - $74,999 ☐

3. $75,000 - $99,999 ☐

4. $100,000 - $124,999 ☑

5. $125,000 - $149,999 ☑

6. $150,000 - $249,999 ☑

4. Targeting Based On Home Ownership Status

Navigate to **Detailed Targeting > Demographics > Home > Home Ownership** *opens the door to three options: renters, homeowners, and first-time homebuyers. The type of properties you sell will decide the portion choose. If you're heavily involved in selling affordable condos, then your target audience should focus mainly on the first-time home buyer.*

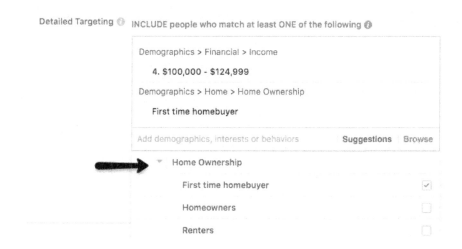

Make your target audience aware that you are on Facebook

This can be done a number of ways. If a lot of your customers have subscribed to your newsletter, then let them know you created a Facebook page. Request that they check it out and follow you. Tell your customers about the nature of the page and the content posted on there, as well as any potential contests and giveaways. Your page will also be an effective means of contact that people can use to ask questions about your products and services.

Furthermore, if your business has a website or anything similar, make sure that you link your Facebook page on there for everyone to see. Be careful not to become annoying, but definitely make sure that everyone knows that you have a Facebook page.

If you've been making the right moves with your company and have basic awareness of advertising and marketing your product or service, you'll understand the words "brand awareness".

Brand awareness is what happens when you spread the gospel of whatever product or service it is, you're in the business of selling. People know you're there, what you have to offer, and why they might like to buy it. But brand awareness is a way of thinking about your business that goes well beyond quality. You're selling a quality service or product, but what's the texture of your brand? What's the color? Who are you talking to and what is it that triggers their decision that they want what you've got?

A successful brand keeps certain principles, an identity, and an aura of personality about it. When people think or talk about your brand, they need to connect particular notions to your brand name. You want these notions to be quality goods and services, excellent customer service, friendliness, charitableness, etc. A brand that has a personality will stick with the customers, and it will be harder for them to forget and replace you with the competition.

Being aware of your own brand is the start of making others aware of it and interested in what it represents. This awareness of your brand will also help you pinpoint who your followers should be on Facebook and how likely they are to become your clients.

It boils down to the old "know yourself" wisdom. If you lack a concrete idea of what your business is and where you want to take it in the future, you will have a hard time representing and promoting it effectively. Brands are a lot like people. Those who are self-aware, in touch with both their strengths and weaknesses, know where they are headed and what they want, will show confidence and stability.

Knowing Your Market

Whatever it is that you're selling, you need to know who's most likely to buy it. Have you done your homework? Whether its widgets, hamburgers or acrylic nails, you need to know who your brand is targeted to. That means, essentially, who is most likely to buy what your brand represents.

Doing research can go a long way towards improving the impact of your marketing strategy if you lack the in-depth knowledge of the market you're aiming for. Be sure to identify the demand for your products and services. Find out if people really need what you are selling and why. Inventing need and convincing people to buy something that isn't necessary to have, isn't likely to be successful. It's always best and more feasible to conduct a thorough analysis of the market and respond accordingly.

Some businesses are so powerful that they actually influence the market and make people interested in something they otherwise wouldn't be. This rarely happens though. It's a better idea to adapt to the forces of the market. So, consider your product and listen to your targeted market. Some products are easier to market as their purpose and demographics of interest are fairly obvious.

Acrylic nails are a no brainer. Most people who avail themselves of this service are women. Most of those women are also between certain ages, a certain income level, and perhaps even of certain marital status. Knowing your market is something you should take the time to pin down as part of your business plan. Even if you decide to just fly by the seat of your pants, still take a little time to gather the information needed to define the market you're selling to. Figure out how to make your brand speak to that market. Striking out on Facebook, as I've said, is about data.

So, what's your niche? What corner of the market are you hoping to carve out and service with your business?

Who are you talking to and Where Are They?

Defining your market is about asking the right questions. Where do the people you're hoping to sell to live? Where do they work?

Having a clear idea of who your potential customers are helps you find them and connect.

The smaller the niche, the more effective you will be in connecting with your targets and communicating with them. Certain niches are more tight-knit than others as the number of people who share an interest in them is limited. These are usually much more connected and forming a community within such niches is easier. Therefore, the relationship you build with your customers and followers is likely to be a more personal and committed one.

When you establish a strong relationship with the customers, trust and certain responsibilities come along with it. Chances are that people will really care about the niche in question, so be careful with how you conduct yourself. Establishing a popular page that concerns one of the smaller niches can gather quite a loyal followership that cares a great deal about the quality of your content and products. It's important to be sure that you can consistently deliver quality services, products, or content. It's also crucial to mind the integrity of the page you are managing. What this means is not "selling out" and being careful as to what you are advertising and promoting.

Create the trust your audience is looking for. The tight-knit niches may be the best for making a sale. But if you upset your audience, aren't able to work with their goals and dreams, say something that bothers them or makes them lose trust in you, it is going to be hard to get all of that back.

There are probably a lot of people who fit into your target niche. You just need to be able to find them. Before you go out searching, make a list of all of the demographic features that you are targeting to sell the product or service. Who would purchase your product or service? What do they do for fun? How old are they, what do they like to wear, and who are their friends?

All of these questions are important when setting up your niche. You are responsible for finding these people. If the demographics are wrong, you won't be able reach the targeted audience. Be careful with your goals, reach the right demographics, and you will find plenty of people who would like to purchase from your business.

Facebook Personal Profile Strategies

The following chapter provides key strategies to help optimize professional branding and networking through the use of a personal Facebook profile. Although not an exhaustive list, the tips and tactics discussed here are some of the most valuable on which to focus your efforts at this stage (including, but not limited to, various privacy and security settings). For a review of business Facebook profiles, refer to Chapter four of this book.

Get clear on how your personal profile can support your business objectives

Most people use Facebook only to connect with family and friends, not realizing the numerous business applications it offers as well. Before applying the specific strategies in this Chapter, get clarity on how using a Facebook profile can support your business objectives. For most business professionals, the greatest benefit is networking

- ith both valuable new business contacts as well as current connections

- hrough sharing interesting pictures, videos, and articles that can further enhance their brand.

The benefits of using a personal Facebook profile correctly for professional aims include:

- Improved professional network

- Improved reputation among other professionals in your sector

- Opportunity to share valuable information related to your company and products

Set aside time to think over your business objectives and specific aspects you'd like your Facebook profile activity to support.

Keep your profile up-to-date

Tools like Facebook are only as good as the information the user provides. Try to keep your profile information current and include all of the relevant information you want people to know. If your Facebook profile is used for both personal reasons and business networking, avoid sharing too much personal data, such as who your family members are or where you live.

Many employers are in the habit of now investigating candidates' Facebook profiles. Whether you're in the market for new work or expanding your network, it's important to share correct and updated professional information (including past experience and skills). Your personal page can share contact details and links to your professional website and other social networks, along with a short introduction about who you are as a business professional.

Facebook pages are tracked by username, so you may wish to revise the default hyperlink assigned to your name. You can do so by visiting www.facebook.com/username and selecting a preferred alternative.

Optimize your privacy settings

As a basic matter, every Facebook user should review and update his or her privacy settings, found at: *www.facebook.com/settings*. These can be customized to your personal preferences; including what other Facebook users have access to viewing. Currently Facebook allows configuration of three different sections:

- Who can see my content?
- Who can contact me?
- Who can look me up?

As a business professional, if you want to maximize promotion of a personal brand, the broadest category is to allow everyone to view every post (in the "who can see my stuff" section). You can also allow search engines to generate links to the profile (in the "who can look me up" section). For safety reasons, be sure to review and restrict personal information on your page, especially since you are providing broad access. On the contrary, privacy settings can also be optimized more openly for those who connect primarily with personal and family members.

It's important to note that Facebook frequently updates and revises the site's privacy terms and settings. I advise visiting these sections every month to confirm that all of the settings are configured according to your preferences.

Facebook Business Page Strategies

Most small and medium-sized businesses need a Facebook Page for marketing and brand presence. However, many businesses utilizing this service struggle to do so properly. They fail to obtain the results to best support the company's business objectives because they are not using the right strategies. The organic reach of a Facebook page is diminishing these days. This is due largely in part to greater competition and oversaturation of the News Feed; Facebook page posts are being seen by less people, requiring greater strategic effort to compensate.

Recently, Facebook paid advertising has become more popular to expand the marketing reach (covered in the next chapter). In this Chapter, you will learn simple yet powerful strategies, which may be implemented prior to paying for such advertising – tactics currently known and utilized by only a few companies – which may be applied to gain greater engagement and better results from Facebook business pages.

Understand it's not about you, it's about them

It's common to see Facebook business Pages with a lot of content, but minimal audience comments, likes, or shares. Pages such as these have nearly zero impact on a business's marketing and are often a waste of the company's time in maintaining. To effectively market your Facebook Page with these services, post content that is interesting from your audience's point of view. It's all about what your Page followers want to hear, not about what you want to say.

Here are few examples to better illustrate this point:

- Instead of giving a call to action to buy something, it's better to say something like, "Would you like to test this?"

- Instead of using the word "we" (as a company), use the word "you" (referring to the follower).

- Instead of talking about what is happening in your company, share posts related to what is happening in the lives of your followers. For example, during Christmas time share posts about the holidays; during summer holidays, share posts about those events.

To get yourself started, create a list of 10 different posts you can make using the above points. You will quickly see that there are many creative ways to utilize the new focus in reaching your audience.

In addition, consider posting a survey to directly ask your customers what kind of content they would like to see on your Facebook page.

Take advantage of Facebook's mobile direction

Smart business owners are already optimizing their Facebook content for mobile devices. However, most businesses are far behind in this market and believe that most of their customers visit Facebook on computers.

The following tips will help you start optimizing your Facebook content for mobile devices:

- Make the text on your post easy to read by using short paragraphs and questions.
- Make sure photos, promotions and other text are all being seen correctly on a mobile device.
- When creating videos, make them short and mobile-friendly.
- Create a QR-code to enable customers to quickly follow your Facebook Page from their mobile devices.
- Visit other Facebook pages to find businesses in your sector and analyze how well their posts and content is viewable from your mobile device.

Download the latest version of the **"Facebook Pages Manager"** app. With this app, you can quickly and easily post photos and updates, view and respond to messages, and view page insights. If your employee manages or uploads content to your Facebook page, have them download and use this application. Doing so will help save time and to post content more effectively.

Avoid the mistakes your competitors are making

Imagine how powerful it would be to see the mistakes your competitors or other companies in your industry are making. Thanks to a variety of tools now available for download, that is now possible. Keep reading to find out how to create powerful Facebook content plans and quickly achieve great results.

Here's how this works in practice, using the free online tool at *www. Likealyzer.com*. Suppose your business is an Italian restaurant in New York and you want to learn from your competitors' mistakes. After doing research, find the Facebook Pages for three local competitors. Next, go to *www.likealyzer.com* and type in the Facebook URL of each of the competitors' pages. Then click "enter" to start the analysis.

Likealyzer.com will provide a specific list of actions that could improve each Facebook page – actions you can take to improve your own restaurant's Facebook page.

The following image shows the recommendations Likealyzer gives on how to improve the page.

I recommend printing out the results and recommendations, visiting and analyzing the competitors' Facebook pages, and finally utilizing the site's recommendation to improve upon your own page. To get more creative ideas, do the same analysis for Facebook pages from other industries and see what kinds of text and content they use.

Improve the engagement of your Page

Engagement is the most important keyword for Facebook Page administrators and is something businesses need to focus on more.

Here is a list of basic strategies to improve the engagement of your Facebook Page:

- Start your Facebook post with a question. If you are posting a picture, it's also possible to embed the question in the image. This helps people viewing your post on mobile devices see the questions better. If sharing a lengthy post, use a question at the end as well. Ask for your followers' opinions by posing two options and asking which one they like better.

- Answer each comment or question on your Page quickly; use a friendly and spontaneous tone. Have fun and use humor in your posts.

- Post statements that would be highly relevant for your followers. A Facebook Page for tennis players could post an emotional statement about how one feels after playing a good game (it's recommended to use a good image for this kind of post). Then, the user could ask people to share the post if they agree, or comment if they disagree.

- Post more photos.

Aside from the above, consider creating more professional photos for your page using online tools, such as *www.Canva.com.* Such free online tools often offer templates that can modified and changed to fit your needs. Spending time creating beautiful visuals will significantly increase the likelihood of fans sharing and engaging in your content. After utilizing these tips when posting for a few weeks, revisit your Facebook Page's insights and analyze which posts have the most engagements. Create more of these kinds of posts in the future.

Constantly trying to improve the engagement and interaction on your Page needs to be the key focus. The more engagement you generate, the more reach Facebook will give you.

Drive local sales using specific promotions

Facebook is becoming increasingly more important for local companies who want to attract new local clients. A common mistake is to invite prospective customers to click on your Facebook Page's "Like" button and expect them to automatically buy your products. Each company needs to consider what kinds of compelling offers they could give to their Facebook followers. The following are some examples that local companies could create for customers who connect on Facebook.

- Restaurants could offer a free desert.

- Chiropractic professionals could offer a first session for free.

- Coaching professionals could offer a free report or first session.

I don't typically recommend offering discounts as they may decrease the perceived value of your product. However, companies that offer services as their product may offer a small test or sample, which can actually help build trust and credibility. A large portion of prospective customers who accept such tests and samples stick around and become actual paying clients.

When creating a special offer for your Facebook fans, it's recommended to track both the number of contacts and number of sales being generated via Facebook. Business owners need to track the following information in order to get a clear idea of how effective any Facebook promotion is:

- How many customers call you after seeing information about your special offer (make sure your employees ask the customers where they have seen the offer, if you run it on other social media sites simultaneously).
- How many customers contact you via the contact feature on the Facebook Page?
- How many customers send you an email?
- How many customers visit your business?

Key elements of a Real estate landing page

Depending complexity of the lead you are trying to generate, keep the text on your page as simple as possible. If the visitor receives an information overflow, they are not likely to become a lead. Keep the text simple but include strong arguments, selling points, and conclusions as to why the visitor should choose your product/ service.

Headline is one of the first things the visitor will read. A nice headline is something describing your service – a great headline will explain how your service will benefit the potential lead.

Social proof is important for lead collecting as well, not just when selling products. People are going to want to see what your previous clients think of your services. (Only include testimonials from clients whom have positive things to say). Depending on the number of clients you've had, there are a bunch of different ways you can do this. Testimonials are a great way.

Video is another way you could use to explain your services. Some people are visual and want to see a video. Some people like to read and want to read about your services. Provide content for both of these people. Have a short video of yourself or a colleague, explaining your services. Remember to include unique selling points, arguments etc., in your video.

Call to action is also one of the most important elements of your lead generating landing page. Make the action you want the visitors to take as easily accessible as possible. Want them to contact you? Have a contact form besides your text. I've seen great results with a simple button named something similar to "Contact me". Upon clicking this button, the visitor can type in a name, e-mail and/or phone number. This will allow your visitor to become a lead easily and quickly.

They want to something for free when using your services

Chances are, you will have competition in your business industry. To easily make your business stand out, offer something for free. When talking about e-commerce, you could offer a 15% discount on the customer's first purchase.

Testing your landing page

There are many reasons to test a landing page, but the main goal is to try and increase the conversion rate. The higher your conversion rate, the more visitors will actually buy something or become a lead. The great thing about achieving a higher conversion rate is that it will effectively increase the conversion rate on all of your traffic sources.

I highly recommend testing your landing pages constantly in order to achieve maximum profitability. Luckily, it is not a difficult task.

A/B testing your landing pages

The most common way to test your landing pages is to do A/B tests. Simply test landing page A against landing page B. Then make a conclusion as to which one works the best and has the highest conversion rate. When A/B testing landing pages, do not make a completely different landing page. If you make multiple pages, you won't know what made one better than the other. You want to have data backing up your decision.

There are many elements of a landing page to run tests on. A successful test will most likely show a landing page with a higher conversion rate. If there isn't sufficient data to back that up, there is the option to look at other factors. Have the bounce rates decreased? If yes, then visitors are spending more time on your landing page, which essentially proves that your new landing page is more engaging.

Elements to test

These are the main elements, which you could test on your landing pages, in order to try and get a higher conversion rate.

Headline

Usually on lead pages, the headline on e-commerce product pages will describe the product at hand. Testing the headline on landing pages is a great strategy to collect leads. If your headline describes your services briefly, test it against a landing page which explains in detail how your service resolves an issue. If you already have a headline explaining how your service resolves an issue, test it against a different headline, explaining how it solves a different issue. Maybe more people are having the issue your new landing page describes.

The call to action button

You can test different text variations on your call to action button. But don't take the meaning away from the button. The visitors must know that by clicking this button, they are engaging in the process of using your service or buying your product. Don't trick them into it because they will notice. If you have a button with the text "Contact us now", you could try and change it to "Reach us", "Let us contact you", or something similar. If you are providing free assessments for customers, the button could say "Get free assessment", which is common for many service providing companies.

Another thing to test on your call to action button is the color. Yes, something so simple as the color. The color on the call to action button should stand out a lot from the background, making it impossible to miss. Try to run tests with landing pages, having different colors on the buttons.

Test the design of the button also. Is it a rounded-square shape now? Test it out with a hard-shaped square, or maybe a circle. Your creativity sets the limit.

Product image or video

A big factor in whether a visitor wants to buy your product or service is how you describe it. If you have a video on your landing page, test it against another landing page with a different video where your product is explained in a similar, yet different way.

With product images, there are many things to test. Experiment with a different picture as the default. Try a different zoom-option or maybe even add a small video of your product in use.

Get the most out of your visitors

You have probably worked hard to get visitors and maybe even are paying to get them. Try to get as much out of them as possible, even the ones who don't end up as a customer or client. There are a few ways to do that.

Collect and see the data your visitors are generating

One important thing to do for your website is install Google Analytics. As you continue to get more and more data, Analytics will help improve your website. Set up a lot of different goals and find out where to improve your site, in order to make more compelling to visitors.

Remarketing

Google AdWords allows you to create a remarketing tag. If you implement it on all sites of your website, you will build a list off all your visitors (in AdWords). Later on, you can advertise to them in different ways, remarketing for display, and remarketing for search. The way it works, is that whenever someone visits your website, the remarketing tag will give the visitors browser a Cookie, to remember who the visitor was.

Collect e-mail addresses

Collecting email addresses is also a very effective way to utilize as many visitors as possible. Encourage them to sign up for your newsletter. When done correctly, it proves to be a very profitable form of marketing. Eventually, there is the possibility to advertise your products to thousands of people, with just a single e-mail. Imagine if you have a conversion rate of 5%. How many purchases is that?

CHAPTER FIVE: INSTAGRAM

If considering this medium, you've effectively acknowledged one key thing: Instagram is a basically imperative interpersonal organization. The photograph sharing application is not just critical for retailers, eateries, or travel organizations but also is well known as a standout amongst the best brand-building instruments accessible today. Instagram is extremely important for every type of business. Instagram is currently a center point, where normal individuals find and judge the visual personality of a business. Without the use of Instagram, organizations are in danger of being disregarded or overlooked, particularly among the up and coming era of buyers. Among American teenagers, Instagram is viewed as the absolute essential interpersonal organization.

Using Instagram could open a universe of chance for your image. Instagram is considered the king of social connection because of its contribution to improving the quality and fame of business. Brands that advertise on Instagram, receive 58 times more engagement for every devotee than Facebook, and 120 times more engagement for each supporter than Twitter.

Now you know why your business should be on Instagram. Next, I'll explain the procedure of building an Instagram system, setting up your record, and best practices for brands. Keep reading to find out the procedure to enhance your business using Instagram.

Use High Quality Pictures (camera: 1080 x 1080):

- When reposting viral pictures, find the source (the photographer's Instagram) of the photo in order to get the highest quality picture!

- When creating content, use good equipment. Don't use apps that crop the picture because this causes the picture to lose quality

Reason:

Instagram's algorithm always favors higher quality content. By posting high quality content over low quality content, you'll have a higher chance of getting good engagement on your post!

Beginning with the application

To begin using Instagram, download it to your cell phone from the Apple Store or Google Play (it's free). Joining this social networking site implies picking an expert email and a safe secret key. Upon entering the application, you'll be incited to round out your profile. Take the time required to improve it and round it out professionally.

Instagram is one of the most straightforward informal communities with regards to your bio. For discoverability, your username should coordinate with the username of your other marked online networking profiles. For this situation, your genuine name is the organization name. The other data that shows up on your open profile is your site (a URL, which you can change to advance crusades or new bits of substance) and a short, 150-character bio. Since the length of your bio is restricted, keep things clear and genuine. Clarify what your business is and what individuals can anticipate from your Instagram profile. Keep it light and smart. The bio could also incorporate any marked hashtags you need devotees to utilize.

Create Instagram Strategy

Begin by doing some exploration. Use Instagram yourself, before utilizing it for your business image. Look at the best organization on Instagram and different business in your industry, including rivals, both for motivation and focused knowledge. Once acquainted with the application, start to fabricate your Instagram technique. This procedure should reflect your more extensive online networking promoting arrangement, which is your business' aide for social networking exercises.

To begin, build up your Instagram objectives. These objectives ought to attach back to your business objectives. They may include:

- Expand item deals
- Expand activity to your site
- Expand brand mind fulness
- Use of hashtag

The objectives set for your Instagram methodology need to be achievable and quantifiable. For instance, don't set an objective to expand your white paper downloads on the off chance that you can't attach your Instagram exercises to your white papers (indicate: this would be truly hard and likely wouldn't work). By making objectives that are quantifiable, you additionally permit yourself to keep tabs on your development, which we'll talk about in more detail.

When recognizing your objectives, create a statement of purpose for your Instagram account. A statement of purpose is a directing standard for your Instagram exercises and will deter you from treating the informal community like Twitter or Facebook. On Instagram, the system's power is in visuals, as your statement of purpose and objectives should mirror.

After clarifying your statement of purpose, move onto your substance procedure. This will include:

- Picking how regularly to post
- Picking what time of day topmost
- Setting up a substance schedule
- Picking your substance topics

Keep up a customary posting plan on Instagram. However, do not besiege your supporters with excessively numerous posts. Most brands discharge one to three posts for every day. Moreover, see the appropriate time of each day to post as this will rely on upon your gathering of people. For both of these elements, recurrence and time, it comes down to testing. Test posts at various interims and times to see what works best. This will rely on upon where your groups of onlookers are found, including their time zone, among different variables. Utilize the knowledge to build up a substance date-book. Your timetable shows who is accountable for posting, when they'll post, and what the substance will be.

Calendar is a new feature available on Instagram. Using the calendar feature spares time on posting each day. This permits you to spend more time on engagement and group building. Invest a touch of energy every week booking your Instagram pictures, at your group of onlookers' most dynamic times.

Building a kick-ass Instagram account is not something you can achieve overnight, but you know, nothing is impossible, I'll like to think that you know all the typical "using a bot service" or 'buying likes' trick. These tricks can be tempting, but in the long run, they will obstruct your long-term ambitions 98% of the time.

The truth is, there is no easy way get a head start on social media and grow your business. I'll admit that getting your page the momentum and traction can be quite aggravating and frustrating in the beginning. It can get to the point that you would think "Why shouldn't I get some help if there is any to make it faster."

The usual suspects are:

CHAPTER FIVE: INSTAGRAM

1- Buying Likes

HERE'S THE THING; Instagram might look like an ordinary photo-sharing app, there's much more in the background that you should be aware of. After that, you'll realize these shortcuts aren't useful at all.

Instagram's algorithm makes use of engagement to show your contents to a bigger audience, that is, the more organic comments and likes you get, the bigger your engagement is and the likeness of your post getting to the Discover page, exposing you to a broader audience.

Keep the word 'engagement' in mind because you'll need it when you're trying to increase your audience.

The first problem with buying likes is that it won't increase your engagement. You're merely buying empty and fake likes. There are no real or organic followers behind the accounts. They're just numbers.

Using this trick will ultimately become a trap since you have to keep up the numbers in your posts. The worst thing is, these fake accounts will not promote or buy your product or service, unlike the real accounts that will help to increase the long-term success of your business.

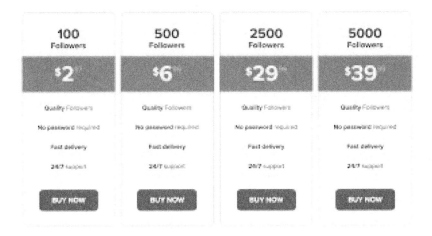

2- Buying Bots to Increase Followers

One of the unspoken things in Instagram is the "Follower loyalty." This means I expect to be followed back when I follow you.

One advantage to buying a bot is that it follows accounts that are relevant and would be interested in following back. After some time, the bot unfollows any accounts that do not follow back. It sounds, but the thing is, the bot will only do what you tell it to.

For example, if you program your bot to comment "Great!" on every post with the word "happy" in the caption. It's all well and great until the bot starts commenting great on posts grieving someone that make the user happy. Bots don't understand the underlying meaning in language; therefore, there is no way these mistakes can be averted. Your brand might be tagged as insensitive if you are not wary of the implications. This is a PR nightmare.

From the above, you should now be familiar with the most popular ways of buying likes and followers, so here are three reasons why it is a bad idea to buy followers and likes:

1- Terrible Marketing Strategy

Your main focus on social media should be creating an honest and robust relationship between your audience and company. Building a long-term relationship with customers is what pushes them into becoming advocates for your brand.

2- Bid Farewell to your Account

Your account will most likely be deactivated. The Instagram Community Guidelines makes sure that any fraudulent activity leads to suspension of your account. Instagram hunts down any user accounts that spam follows and comments without the honest mode of engagement, this, therefore, leads to deactivation of thousands of accounts.

3- Kiss your Engagement Goodbye

The number of likes per post on Instagram is not the priority, but rather how many likes you get in respect to the number of followers you have. The lesser the likes you have from your normal followers compared to your fake followers will result in a lower engagement which ultimately stops your post from showing in everyone's timeline.

Using shady activities to gain popularity on Instagram will do more harm than good. Funny this is, it does quite the opposite of what you have in mind. So, try to grow your account the healthy way, aim to gain loyal and organic followers, and sit back and watch both your business and engagement rise at the same time.

Have you ever seen someone pushing you to buy Instagram followers cheaply? It must be quite tempting especially if you're looking to make it as an influencer. An easy way to increase your Instagram clout without having to work for it is quite tempting.

But in life, good things don't come easy, and there is always a catch. Buying followers is not the same as getting followers from the quality of your posts. As a matter of facts, buying Instagram followers can lead to some problems, and destroy your online reputation at the same time.

Furthermore:

1. No Engagement For Fake Instagram Followers

Instagram Fake followers are of two types. The first one is the one that goes on a fake followers list for a sum of money. The get added as followers to thousands of accounts without engaging in any of them. They will happily take the money but will not show any interest whatsoever in the accounts they follow. They won't even look at the post.

The second type of fake follower is not even a real person. They are usually a bot masquerading as an Instagram follower. Some of the bots engage, they make automated comments on some posts. But this means nothing, they may be some form of AI, but no deep learning is involved. They are not programmed to learn from your contents.

What's the point of following on a social media if the person does not engage whatsoever? The main purpose of all these online hubs is to create a platform for people to be social.

2. Mismatched Engagement

Humans are relatively predictable. Your human followers will always follow a normal pattern of engagement no matter how important you are. Sometimes, smaller accounts receive more engagement than larger accounts, but there's still a pattern.

> 1 million followers = 1.7% engagement

10,000 – 100,000 followers = 2.4% engagement

< 1,000 followers average = 8% engagement

1,000 – 10,000 followers = 4% engagement

Your engagement might not match these numbers because they are estimates. But they should be around these percentages.

With fake followers, however, yours is odds-on to be in stark contrast to those above. Fake followers do not interact with posts at all and this will reduce your engagement rate.

You should note that any "useless comment" is a type of engagement. Fake account sellers have recognized the engagement problem, and some have created bots that make fake and useless comments to boost engagement rates. So, if you see comments like "nice picture" it is safe to assume they are fake Instagram followers.

3. Likelihood of Spam Followers

If you want to buy followers, you'll get to a point where your email address will be needed. At this point, you just opened yourself to a large amount of spam. A lot of people that sell followers do so to gain your email for spam reasons.

After you accept them as followers, you will give them access to your followers. These followers will accept spammers as followers just because they follow you. Once they find out what was sent to them, your real followers may purge you when they are removing the fake followers.

4. You End up With Useless Comments

People use fake followers boost their engagement rages through irrelevant and inappropriate comments. These comments are worse than "nice picture" comments which also are of little value or truth. In this case, your "followers" will leave irrelevant comments to your posts.

For example, you might notice people promoting some politician in a country you have never been to or sex toys in your image of a beautiful sunset.

These followers often use your post as an advertising medium. In reality, it is of no value to anyone. They are not genuine followers, and they are unlikely to buy any product.

5. Fake Followers are Dud Prospects

Fake followers will not spend any of their money on you. Whether they are real people merely playing the game for money or bot (that does not spend money). They have no interest in you, and they definitely won't spend any of their money on you.

6. Fake Followers Accounts Lack Credibility

Pointing out accounts with fake followers is very easy. It is especially easy for brands and people that use agencies and platforms to assist their influencer selection.

This means that anyone that deliberately buys a follower won't remain an influencer forever. By engaging in this practice, your credibility might be destroyed.

If businesses don't use agency or platforms, and they use any of the software we've highlighted, they will quickly spot that you have fake followers.

Unfortunately, people might start noticing your fake followers, and this will ultimately lead to a loss of credibility as a business or influencer. They will question the ethics of your dealings.

7. Instagram Deletes Fake Followers

Instagram is becoming skillful when it comes to spotting fake followers nowadays. They don't want users to have a fake user experience.

This means money spent on fake followers will be wasted anyhow since fake followers are removed from Instagram one by one.

Tools to Help You Discover Fake Instagram Followers

There is a wide range of paid and free tools that can help you discover if your followers are real or fake, or whether an account has too many fake followers. In recent times, apps like Deep Social have proven to be comprehensive in tracking fake followers and the likes.

Unfortunately, Deep social is commencing a winding down process and will be permanently discontinuing the services very soon. This is as a result of Instagram and Facebook recent privacy changes that make it harder to access information of accounts.

1. Influencer Marketing Hub Instagram Audit Tool

Forget your worries about the credibility of influencers. You can enter your influencer's handle to our free IG Bot Analysis and get access to the credibility of such account.

The tool uses account factors like number of accounts followed to the following ratio, accounts avatar, number of posts, and number of likes ratio to the number of likes received and more to establish the quality of the Instagram account.

A real influencer that worked hard at ensuring the genuineness of their audience should have a score of at least 80 and above.

2. Fakecheck

Follower Audit Result

This account has lower than expected social engagement from likes.

This account has lower than expected social engagement from comments, or comments are disabled.

Likes should average	19,972
Comments should average	940
Likely real followers	29,995 (2.55%)
Possible fake follower	1,144,836 (97.45%)

FakeCheck helps to determine the number of fake followers in your account with a social Engagement check. It does this by collecting data about an account follower engagement level.

The service requires payment. If you search for an account, you can use credits to unlock its report. You can only buy these credits – the cost of the credits reduces the more when you buy them.

3. HypeAuditor

HypeAuditor is another powerful tool that allows users to analyze an Instagram account for any fake likes and followers. This helps users to assess their influencers before they work with them. HypeAuditor does this by providing the accounts with an Audience Quality Score (AQS).

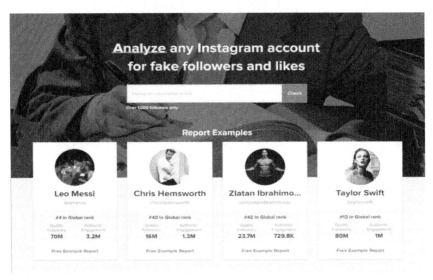

The Audience Quality Score is a score out of 100. It analyzes an account's Engagement Rate, Authentic Engagement, and Followers' Reachability. It uses AI to detect cheating and sporadic followers who will never make a profit for your brand.

Audience Quality Score is out of 100. It uses the Authentic Engagement, Engagement rate, and the followers' reachability to score the account. It also uses an AI to detect sporadic and cheating followers that will not make a profit for your product or service.

You pay for the Instagram report with tokens. 1 token = 1 Instagram report for 1 month. The more the token bought, the cheaper they are. If you're checking a single account, a token with be $1.99

4. Social Audit Pro

Social Audit Pro is an app that allows users to investigate different profile and determine their legitimacy. Prices range from $5 for a one-time audit of 5,000 followers and $20 for 20,000 followers. Larger packages are also available especially if you have higher requirements than the usual package.

You can optionally remove the followers that have been flagged as dormant or fake by Social Audit Pro after auditing your account directly from the application.

5. IG Audit

IG Audit is a tool that can help check on Instagram's account validity. If you're suspicious about your account, you should enter the Username into the IG Audit search box. It will provide an estimate of the percentage of fake followers to real ones.

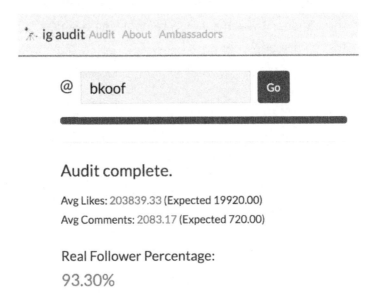

Audit complete.

Avg Likes: 203839.33 (Expected 19920.00)

Avg Comments: 2083.17 (Expected 720.00)

Real Follower Percentage:

93.30%

It also shows the account's average likes and comments (along with expected figures for each statistic). It will also show the average likes and comments of the account (plus the expected figures for every post)

Boost The Organic Reach of Your Brand with Engagement Groups

As we have seen so far in this book, Instagram can play a significant role in marketing. In this subchapter, we will extensively discuss an Instagram growth strategy that is not usually covered in typical marketing writeups.

Also known as Instagram Pods, engagement groups on Instagram can be used to increase the number of organic followers that interact with your brand.

Whether you're just starting to learn about how to promote your real estate business on Instagram or you're a professional real estate broker, chances are that you haven't even heard about Instagram Engagement Groups.

First of all, you should know there are dozens of ways to drive up the engagement of your real estate business to get more listings. In my opinion, the ones that know the most of these practices are the ones that are crushing it.

Instagram is one of the fastest and hottest social media platforms. It has over 600 million monthly active users in the platform at the start of 2017 (according to statista.com). However, only 5% of US small businesses are on Instagram for their usual online marketing service. This means, it is yet to be saturated, and users are not likely to get noticed.

What are Engagement Groups?

The primary purpose of using an engagement group is to integrate your real estate business posts into Top posts section and increase your organic growth from there. Instagram Engagement groups are like simple group conversations with Instagram and other platforms. They are called engagement groups because people participate for the sole purpose of liking and/or commenting on a post in exchange for their posts getting commented and/or liked.

All groups have rules. It might either be a comment only group, like-only group, or the combination. There are also cases of groups forming around Instagram stories. Since it's a new feature on IG, people are still experimenting on how story engagement aids account growth.

Most of the time, there is usually a particular for users to drop their posts in the group so it can get comments and likes at the first hour of posting. This is usually a good indicator that helps Instagram to rank contents.

In an engagement group, the specific time when all members post their comments is called rounds. A round is usually brief, and it starts 30 minutes after engagement time. This is the stipulated time for users to drop their usernames in the conversation.

After 30 minutes, users will not be able to drop their usernames, and the list of all users participating will be compiled by the chatbot. After this, participants can start their engagement as seen below:

When you're done engaging with all the posts, it is usually required in the group to announce that you're done. This depends on the regulations and rules of the group.

Groups can also work asynchronously. This means all members can drop posts into groups whenever they want and comment on other posts whenever they want.

A typical example is the comment group. You open the group, drop comments on the latest posts in the groups, and join in the conversation. If anybody else wants to participate, he/she will comment on the last five posts and drop his/her own.

Both options work fine as they achieve the intended goal of getting real people to interact with your posts. However, to get massive growth, it's better if you can plan the time for higher engagement. As I said before, it's essential to get a lot of engagement in the first hour of posting.

These options are okay as long as real people like and comment on your posts. However, to get a massive growth, you need to plan your time for higher engagement. As mentioned earlier, it is crucial to attract massive engagement within the first hour you put up the post.

What Impact do Engagement Groups have on Real Estate Business?

Just as things change in life, Instagram regularly changes its algorithm and ranking factors. In 2016, a lot of users were tagging popular accounts like (@selenagomez, @cristiano and others) in their caption which attracted huge engagement numbers. It was commonplace to see accounts gain thousands of followers overnight by optimizing a viral video with famous account tags.

This approach does not work anymore. Even though there is the possibility that if one of these famous accounts likes or comments on your posts, it will boost your ranking, it is implausible that these famous accounts will interact with your post.

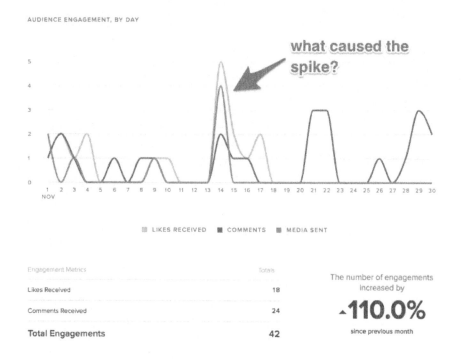

AUDIENCE ENGAGEMENT, BY DAY

■ LIKES RECEIVED   ■ COMMENTS   ■ MEDIA SENT

Engagement Metrics	Totals
Likes Received	18
Comments Received	24
Total Engagements	**42**

The number of engagements increased by

▲**110.0%**

since previous month

This strategy works now and should for the considerable future. With top-notch content and well-researched hashtags, you can get your posts into the Top Posts categories. So, take advantage of this method while you can.

Also, recently there have rumors swirling that comments and likes that originate from group conversations in Instagram messages are not as valuable as likes and comments from external sources.

Generally, on Instagram and other platforms, likes are less valuable than comments. However, this might depend on factors like follower count, location, engagement, and account type (personal vs. business).

How can I Join the Relevant Engagement Groups?

For niches like real estate, these engagements groups are not heavily promoted, so the logical step is to reach out to accounts that are attracting massive engagement numbers and inquire about their participation in any engagement groups so that you can join too.

While the majority of these groups are free, others require entrance free (watch out for scammers).

Engagement groups pretty much work the same. The trick is to identify groups where the members post similar content and have the same follower count on average. This will help you eliminate the risk of attracting engagement from random accounts with small follower counts.

You can also use search engines like Google and Bing to find engagement groups, but the best place to start is Instagram groups and Telegram groups. If you are having difficulty finding the relevant engagement groups for your niche, be sure to contact me on Instagram @sebastianacosta. It would be my pleasure to link you with the appropriate groups and point you in the right direction.

Instagram engagement groups are the hottest trends these days – the hard part is identifying and gaining an invite to one. Thankfully, you are reading this book, and I will teach you how to find and join the most relevant engagement groups.

In this subchapter, I will also be exploring the intricacies on how Instagram engagement groups work, and with this knowledge, you can even create an Instagram engagement group. Engagement groups are tailored to promote your engagement levels, go viral, regularly get features on the Instagram Explore page, and gain thousands of new followers in your niche. But as Rome wasn't built in a day, achieving these milestones require patience, dedication, and lots of hours to achieve your desired result.

Types of Instagram Engagement Groups

1. DM Groups

A typical Instagram engagement group works in a simple way, where every member notifies the group whenever they publish a post on Instagram. This notification is communicated through a group DM. Once the member notifies the other members, they are obligated to like and comment on the post as soon as they can.

Every engagement group has its own set of rules about engagements, but usually, every member of the group must have liked and commented on the current post before they post one of their own to the group.

The comments and likes from other group members will undoubtedly boost engagement and promote visibility on your Instagram post, which will lead to your account gaining more followers.

How to find Instagram DM groups in your niche: You have two solid options namely: ask big accounts on Instagram or check out Facebook groups. Simply identify Instagram-related Facebook groups – majority of them post a weekly thread for new users who want to join or form their own Instagram engagement group. You will find someone in your niche and join their group or post a listing to find members of your group.

2. Instagram Rounds Engagement Groups on Telegram

A Rounds engagement group on Telegram follows the same template as the regular Instagram engagement group, but with some key differences. Telegram rounds groups are created inside the Telegram app (just like WhatsApp and Kik) as a group chat. Depending on the group, members can vary from hundreds to thousands in numbers.

Members post at specified times, instead of sporadically in a Telegram rounds group. It uses a concentrated mode of engagement. For example: If your engagement group has 200 members with a Round scheduled at 7 pm, you will get 200 new likes on one of your Instagram posts, starting at 7 pm.

You are expected to reciprocate by liking 200 posts too – for each group member. This must be completed within an hour to help every member achieve the best result. Majority of Telegram engagement groups schedule rounds for every day of the week. You get to pick which rounds you want to partake in, without any obligation to catch up on any rounds you missed later.

Where can I find Telegram Engagement Groups?

This website *https://telegram.me/engagementgroups* is a directory that links you to a Telegram round group in your niche. All you need to do is create a Telegram account to access the directory. It contains a regularly updated list of Telegram engagement groups, and each group has its own specific sets of instructions and information on who to contact before you can get accepted into the group.

fter getting accepted into a group, make sure you respect the rules of the group and ask questions if you are unsure about anything. Group members are not fond of "leeches" who are quick to drop their username to garner likes and comments without supporting the rest of the group. You will likely be kicked out of the group if you don't adhere to the rules of engagement.

DM groups or Telegram Engagement Groups?

DM groups are effective but not as much as Telegram rounds engagement groups for many reasons:

The amount of engagement you get on a post within minimal time determines your ranking in Instagram's algorithm. The higher your levels of engagement, the wider your reach, which will help your account grow faster. So, a bigger group usually guarantees bigger results, and by getting your group to receive likes and comments fast, you ate increasing its influence.

If you receive high engagement in a short time, your post can get featured on the Instagram Explore Page. And what are the benefits of making it to the Instagram Explore Page? Below is

You get an insane number of likes, comments, and views! Significant boosts in engagement like these will eventually lead to an increase in follower growth like these:

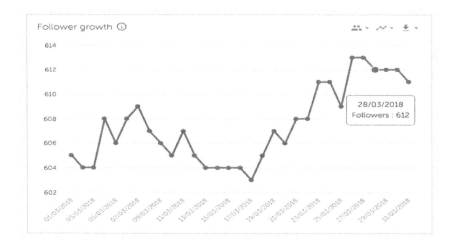

Why does this happen?

If one of your posts is featured on the Instagram Explore Page, it will be viewed by a much larger audience compared to your usual engagement numbers. Your post also has the possibility of going viral especially if you post scintillating and relatable content that cut across niches – which can result in engagement numbers like those shown above.

The reason why typical Instagram DM engagement groups cannot attract high numbers like these are:

- Likes and comments are sporadic which is ineffective when it comes to boosting content on the page.
- Instagram DM groups have a cap of 15 people. So, the highest number of engagements you can expect is 15 likes/ comments. Round s groups, on the other hand, are much bigger and will help you achieve a better result.

An alternative option to make your Instagram DM groups more effective is to join more than one. Say, you're in 10 DM groups, you

can get up to 150 likes and comments on posted content. The only downside to this option is you might not get engagement on your post all at once. But if there are large accounts in the same niche as you on your DM groups, they can be very useful in promoting your profile to the Instagram Explore Page.

Apart from Instagram engagement groups, it is important to have a proven Instagram growth strategy to grow your follower count consistently. A lot of methods and tactics are very effective in giving your business more exposure on Instagram. To some extent, this same tactic that I will be sharing below have proven to be efficient on Snapchat. This is because of the recent rise of "stories" on social media.

Gain Exposure and Promote Visibility with Instagram Location Stories

One of the most fun and effective methods to increase awareness of your brand and simultaneously grow your Instagram account is the

Instagram Stories function. It is possible to gain targeted exposure and deliver your content to a broader audience through Instagram Stories. In this section, we will take a look at how to use this feature to increase your brand's exposure.

Why Use Instagram Location Stories?

Simply put, they are a great way to increase local exposure for your business on Instagram. Businesses that have a physical location, or in cases of real estate, where properties and listings are in a specific area, can benefit immensely from Instagram Location Stories.

With the aid of location tag search, new users can discover your story and the content you are trying to promote.

Location stickers are an effective way to get your story into the midst of larger location stories which can be discovered on the Explore feed.

Getting Noticed With The Use Of Location Stickers

Location stickers are categorized into two: literal location stickers allow users to tag a physical address in their story. The lesser-known option is the city-specific stickers which pop up based on your location.

That's right. Not only do they show your followers the city you're based but also other functions. When you click on them, they lead to a larger location story that is featured on the Explore page. Just imagine the amount of engagement you can attract with the extra views on your story.

Adding location sticker to your Instagram story is relatively easy. Just follow the steps below:

- Take photo, boomerang, or video.
- Select the "sticker" icon. It is the smiley face on the top right corner of the screen.
- Click on the "Location" feature or the aesthetically pleasing city sticker
- The sticker will appear on your screen, and you can click on it to customize.

Additionally, location hashtags and hashtags stickers are very influential in attracting engagement. n. Using hashtags on Instagram is a very effective way to attract engagement and boost your brand's exposure on Instagram.

Best Ways to Use Instagram Location Stories

Now that you are caught up on how to make lotion stories work for your brand, you need to learn the best way to put this essential tool to practice.

1. At events

If you frequently attend real estate industry events, be sure to share Instagram location stories from the gathering. It helps your followers know how the business works behind the scenes.

2. To highlight local happenings

If you own a local business, it can be very effective to take note of events and gatherings that are happening in your city. This will help you connect with local prospects and opens an avenue for a larger audience. Imagine the kind of exposure your brand can get by creating Instagram locations stories that are optimized with the relevant local hashtags and location stickers.

3. Tag your location

It is important to remember that your own business needs its own Instagram location story. Simply combine a local hashtag or location sticker with tags on your location. You can elicit the right   response from your audience because anyone who searches your location will see your story.

3. Add poll stickers to your Instagram location stories

It's a smart idea to combine Instagram poll stickers with location stickers. Using both features in your location stories is very useful because your target audience can ask questions about a specific location. This is a very attractive way to boost your engagement, especially in the real estate business.

4. Connect with other location stories creators in your niche

Lastly, another important method to use location stories to your advantage is by watching stories in your niche and city. By connecting with fellow brands and users in your town or city, you can increase your brand awareness.

Instagram as an app is an impressive digital marketing tool loaded with features, like Instagram location stories, that are tailored to promote awareness and engagement for any business. You should consider utilizing this function on the platform to get prospects and convert them to leads or paying customers.

How to do Successful Instagram Paid Advertising Posts by Creating a Sales Funnel Page

Funnel With Instagram Ads

Instagram is used by up to 32% of Internet users, according to Pew Research Center's 2016 Social Media Update. Any serious brand can achieve success with the help of an active Instagram page with decent following numbers.

But that's not the whole key to success. Sure, every article hypes up Instagram and its brand-building ability. But, to further create a successful online presence for your brand, an important key is to use paid advertising as a sales funnel.

What is a Social Sales Funnel?

Social selling has become an essential tool for marketing teams that want to interact with prospects. With social selling, marketers can use social media to build an interactive channel with potential customers.

It is an effective way to achieve personal and business goals.

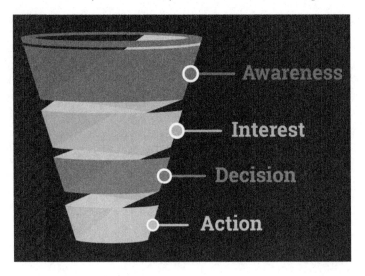

An effective social media sales funnel involves you or your sales team providing a series of content that attracts a prospect and converts them to a paying customer.

Through social media, you can contact potential buyers who can respond to your content at their own time. This is a stark contrast to hard sells and disruptive cold calls. However, Instagram does not always have to be at the top of the sales funnel.

While Instagram and other platforms like Facebook favor a top-of-the-page funnel, Pinterest Buy prefers the bottom.

Creating social media sales funnel does not have a template or predefined rules. It explores the whole spectrum of the buying process. Every view, reply, direct message, and sale is covered from advocacy to awareness. Social media can, therefore, replace traditional sale funnels in this regard. And the buying process is online-based now.

With social media, customers can be expressive with how and when they purchase goods or services. Sales do not have to be linear like the traditional sales funnel propagates.

Below is an excellent example of how social media sales funnel should look like.

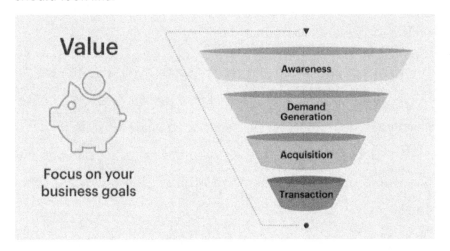

The steps of interaction do not have to follow the same order at all times, however. For example, a contest (activation) on your page could lead to the discovery of your profile (acquisition) by a serious prospect. It is possible for the client to follow your page (acquisition) and then go straight to a sign-up page (absorption).

A social sales funnel does not prioritize a linear path of actions. It rather enforces a cluster of these actions. A solid way to use your

Instagram page as a social media sales funnel is through contests. Let me explain how.

Increase Leads by Hosting Competitions

Regardless of whether a user is following your brands or personal Instagram page, they will always welcome the chance to win a free prize. To boost your brand's leads, you must learn how to create a lead-building Instagram contest.

So, what are the basics to be learned? Here goes:

To get started, create a giveaway concept based on a specific product you want to promote. In real estate, you are wanting to sell properties and partake in consultations so giving out a free PDF e-book on **How To Buy And Sell Homes** is a good place to start.

Once you have picked your price, you need to pick a simple but catchy hashtag that resonates with your followers' interests, brand, and the competition in a similar way.

Also, you need to decide what type of contest you want to hold. Is it a tag-to-win contest, like-to-win contest, or even a favorite house challenge? Once you have finalized this, you have to write up a list of instructions for users to gain entry to the contest. It is important to create a top-of-funnel metric to ascertain the end goal of the contest.

Finally, make plans for a follow-up. How do you intend to contact the winner? Will you contact them via email or direct message? Will there be a photo op?

"Like to win" contests are very effective if you need to keep your followers active and maintain audience participation. It increases engagement but has zero effect on lead generation or brand awareness.

On the other hand, "Tag to win" contests are the best at generating the highest amount of ROI.

A classic example is the giveaway by Meraki Travel Company to celebrate 1000 followers. The brand did a giveaway of three Meraki kits for their worldwide audience.

If possible, create an Instagram carousel to promote your giveaway. This is useful if there are multiple products that you want to give away.

Another option is to create another page for your followers to sign up so that you can track the number of people that click on the link. This option represents a great way to gather more email subscribers for newsletters and promotional emails.

Call-to-actions (CTAs) are very effective and should be added to the captions of your giveaway posts. Popular CTAs include "Comment on this post and tag two friends" and "Retweet this post." Adding them to your post is bound to boost the level of engagement on your giveaway post.

Finally, keep the instructions concise and succinct. Ideally, the instructions should not involve more than three steps to gain entry into the competition. Keep instructions short and simple. Be sure to include no more than three steps to enter.

Ideally, competitions should be run once a month to give your leads and engagement level time to grow.

Increase Leads By Giving Exclusive Offers

Another alternative to giveaways is to provide exclusive offers on properties and listings to your followers to keep them hooked. Giving your followers' promotions, discounts, and exclusive offers is a wonderful way to promote your Instagram page.

By offering bonuses, discounts, promotions, and insider announcements to your followers, you can attract high engagement. Generally, Instagram users are wired to stay dedicated to brands when special perks are involved.

A prime example is the Starbucks Instagram page where special seasonal drinks are announced to inform customers and increase engagement. With text overlay, you can add crucial information in an aesthetically pleasing way to make the post more appealing.

With the help of apps like Over and Phonto, users can add a message, in a special font, and position text anywhere on the image. Canya is another tool that can achieve the same result. You can even add shapes, frames, text, icons, and more to the images make use of Canya's stock images.

Apart from the above-mentioned features, you can select from the default templates to use as overlaying custom text. Next, consider adding a CTA or link to your bio. Ideally, it should follow this format.

Since Instagram does not allow space for a lot of links and text, you have to make the most of what is available.

A good way to achieve this is by adding a CTA to your bio that refers your followers back to your website, store, or product landing page.

A good example is my own Instagram bio that includes a link alongside the CTA that reads "Buy, Sell, and Invest"

If you have a new property or book you want to promote, add a CTA and link in your bio to guide followers to a more detailed page containing relevant information to your brand.

Focus your efforts on making your posts personal. Nobody likes to see the same old generic format. Include sneak peeks of your services and properties. Include behind-the-scenes shots of your brand at work. Don't shy away from promoting a personal feel to your brand.

Contrary to popular opinion, steps like these are not unprofessional at all. They are necessary if you want to cultivate good customer relationships and boost sales. Users always want to feel connected to the brand they are purchasing from when they purchase goods or services online. Instagram helps them to achieve that.

Your followers and prospects want to know about your business, your services, and even your employees. Posting personal photos from time to time is a good way to let your followers know about the brains behind the brand.

Include shots of meetings with your employees or with clients. Take it up a notch by posting pictures of the whole gang grabbing after-work drinks.

With personal posts and sneak peeks, your followers can follow every deal you close and feel like a part of the company. This also allows your brand to show potential customers your consultation services and the type of deals you work on.

Don't just include photos of properties and related content, Instagram should not act as a catalog of services you render, even if it is a platform for social sales.

Look to motivate your followers with inspiring quotes so that your page is not overridden with sales content. With quotes, you do not have to bother about adding the best filter or getting the perfect angle, as you would with pictures

Instagram Ads as a Sales Funnel

Instagram Ads can be found on the Facebook Ads Manager dashboard, which implies that it is possible to sync your Facebook Ads with Instagram Ads. This feature allows you to monitor buyer personas and apply the same targeting options that you have been using on Facebook. Instagram ads operate on a cost per acquisition rate.

You can always adjust your budget to reflect the success of your sales. If you have been closing deals, increase the budget and vice versa.

As mentioned earlier, a good way to use Ads is with Instagram Stories. Instagram stories are not included on your profile or part of your followers' image feed. Rather, they are featured in the "Stories" section and will regularly pop up between the stories feed of your target audience followers.

This makes them unique compared to the usual dramatic ads.

Even NASA (National Aeronautics and Space Administration) make use of Instagram business stories to make citizens feel closer to their projects!

 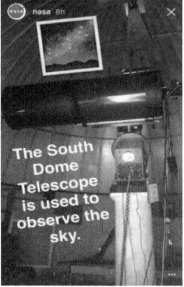

Instagram Feed as a Sales Funnel

Another option for running ads on Instagram is the Instagram Feed Ads feature. Feed Ads appear in your target audience/followers photo feeds. You can use Feed Ads to attract engagement from users with similar interests. The key component for a successful Feed Ads is to make it visually appealing because they are usually integrated between real Instagram posts.

natural clickbait feature to add to these ads is the "Learn more" button that will funnel viewers to your service page.

Now that you have successfully mastered the different process through which you can use Instagram ads as a sales funnel, the next step is to track the numbers. Make sure you monitor the success of your Instagram posts to increase your leads.

The point of creating a social sales funnel through paid Instagram advertising is to attract new leads and convert them into paying customers. The only way to achieve this is to track the growth rate, identify what works, and keep repeating them. Tools like Iconosquare are very effective at tracking relevant data to gauge your social sales success on any platform.

Reciprocity

The number one metric to track is reciprocity. It lets you calculate the number of followers that actively interact with your brand on Instagram. You can see who comments on your images the most, who likes your posts, and users who tag your business the most.

This is important because these followers, in the long run, can become brand ambassadors. With word of mouth, they can boost your exposure through shout outs.

Maintaining a good relationship with your most loyal followers is an important aspect of social sales funnel. These followers are the closest to being) paying customers and must be treated accordingly.

Monitor Engagement Flow to Optimize Your Posting Schedule

Tracking engagement density provides you with data on the days and times when your post gets the highest engagement. SumAll for example, claims that the best time to put up a business post on Instagram is around 6 pm on Mondays. This is a generalized statement that does not apply to every niche, which is why you need to understand your target audience.

As a Real estate broker or agent, the most common time when clients want to buy or sell houses is in Spring or Fall after Labor Day. This piece of information is vital because it helps you to make informed decisions on when to build a social sales funnel page or create paid ads during these periods.

To maximize engagement, plan a posting schedule that will coincide with the booming days and make sure you stick to the schedule.

Post on a Regular Basis

While you want your followers to be conversant with your brand, you need to find the right balance so that your posts don't override their feed. Once you have created a posting schedule and monitored the appropriate density, stick to it. Ensure you upload about two or three images during each peak period.

Do NOT post images within minutes of each other. Also, make sure you put an average of seven posts per week. Research has shown that it will help you grow your engagement level by at least 56% faster with this method.

Most books only discuss the brand-building ability of Instagram. However, it is a very useful tool to drive leads and turn prospects to customers. Follow all the steps highlighted above, make your followers feel connected to your brand, create Feed Ads and Instagram Stories, use tools like Iconosquare to track engagement, and the success of your sales funnel.

Sharing Your Instagram Posts

After applying an optional filter and making edits, the site will direct you to another tab. In this tab, the user can fill out a caption, tag other users, tag a geographic location and simultaneously post to other social networks. Once published, your followers will be able to view your content and interact within their feeds. There is the option to delete or edit details after publishing posts, by tapping the three dots at the top.

Configure your Instagram account to have photos posted on Facebook, Twitter, Tumblr or Flickr. If these sharing configurations are all highlighted, as opposed to remaining gray and inactive, then your Instagram photos will automatically be posted to your social networks after you press Share. If you don't want photos shared on any particular social network, tap the network, so that it turns gray and is set to off.

Viewing and Publishing Instagram Stories

Instagram recently introduced its new Stories feature; a secondary feed that appears at the very top of your main feed. The stories are marked by little photo bubbles of the users you follow. Tap anyone of these bubbles to see that user's story that they have published over the last 24 hours. If familiar with Snapchat, then you'll notice how similar Instagram's stories feature is to it.

To publish your own story, tap your own photo bubble from the main feed or swipe right on any tab to access the stories camera tab. If you want to find out more about Instagram stories, check out this breakdown of how it differs from Snapchat.

TEN TIPS EVERY INSTAGRAM BEGINNER SHOULD KNOW

Instagram is no of the hottest social networks right now. It's visual, it's quick, it's mobile and it's pretty simple to use. There's no better time than now to get started with Instagram. The following 10 tips can help make the best out of your own Instagram experience so you can grow.

1. Post interesting, colorful photos and videos.

Instagram is about providing value to your followers, especially if you want more engagement. Your goal should be to post photos and videos that evoke some kind of emotion - happiness, humor, motivation, nostalgia, love, or anything else. High-quality photos with a lot of colors tend to get the most attention on Instagram.

2. Try not to over do it with the filter effects

Instagram provides many filters you can apply to your photos to automatically enhance the look and style, but that trend seems to have already hit its peak. People favor photos and videos that are colorful, but relatively natural looking. Try to limit your use of filter effects to keep the color and contrast normal in most of your photos.

3. Use hashtags sparingly

Using hashtags is a great way to increase your reach on Instagram, encourage more engagement, and attract new followers. Unfortunately, some people take it way too far. Their captions are often bloated with hashtags, many of which aren't even relevant to the topic of their photo. If you decide to use hashtags, make sure to keep it to a minimum, and only use keywords that are relevant.

4. Use the Explore tab (popular page) to find great new content

The **Explore tab** on Instagram is where some of the most popular photos and videos get featured. The photos shown are tailored, according to the photos and videos that have been liked or commented on, by people you follow. You can find new users to follow or engage with by checking out this tab regularly.

5. Post often to keep followers interested.

If you want to keep followers' engaged, post new contents on regular basis. That doesn't mean post 10 photos a day. In fact, posting once a day or at least once every other day should be frequent enough to keep your current followers interested. If you go long periods without posting, don't be surprised if you lose a few followers.

6. Use Instagram Direct to get into contact with specific users

It's a good idea to post frequently to keep your followers engaged, but it's not always necessary to publicly post something to all your followers. Instead, you can target one or more specific users by privately direct messaging a photo or video. Instagram Direct is a great way to connect with specific groups of users without needing to broadcast your content for everyone to see.

7. Interact with your followers

Never ignore your most loyal followers who regularly like and comment on your photos! That's a surefire way to eventually drive people away. Instead, you want to make your followers feel valued. Reply to their comments or even go check out their account and like few of their photos. You can use a third party tool like Iconosquare (formerly called Statigram), to track comments and see which users are interacting with you the most.

8. Don't be tempted to purchase followers

There's lots of hype around buying Instagram followers and it is true that you can get some big numbers for pretty cheap. The problem with buying them is that the followers are often fake and inactive. Your account may look a little strange to users who see that you have 15K followers, but almost no likes or comments on your photos and videos. Stick to real engagement. It's not all about the numbers.

9. Experiment with shoutouts

Interacting with your current 'followers' is always recommended, but the more people you reach out to, the better. Doing a shout out or s4s with another account in the same follower range is a very fast and effective way to reach more people. Two users basically agree to give the other a shoutout post on their own accounts. This is the main technique that many Instagram users have used to grow their accounts by the thousands.

10. Stay on top of the latest Instagram trends.

Hashtags and shoutouts are great, but even trends like these will   eventually expire. If Instagram is a major social networking platform for you, it's important to keep up with the latest trends, to avoid putting yourself at risk of losing valuable followers. Check out these five big trends that are currently hot on Instagram.

How To Use Instagram's Direct Messaging Feature

1. Get Started with Instagram Direct

If you're on Instagram, chances are you've heard about Instagram Direct, a new built-in private messaging feature. If you're not familiar, these points will provide a brief explanation of what Instagram Direct is.

You no longer have to post everything publicly on Instagram. Getting in contact with somebody is much easier with Instagram Direct. To get started with Instagram Direct, download the app on your mobile device and make sure to have the most current version.

2. Look for Your Instagram Direct Inbox on the Home Feed

Now, with the latest version of Instagram, you should notice a small icon in the very top right corner of the screen on the home feed. Tapping that icon will bring you to your Instagram Direct inbox. Access it any time you want to view or reply to messages.

3. Choose a Photo or Video to Share

The first step in using Instagram Direct is to set up a photo or video, exactly the way as Instagram for public sharing. Simply tap the middle camera button to snap a photo or film a video, or upload an existing one from your camera roll or other folder on your mobile device.

4. Select the 'Direct' Tab at the Top of the Screen

After selecting and editing a photo or video to share, you willbe brought to a familiar page. On this page, you can type your caption, tag friends, choose your location and share your post to other social networking sites.

At the very top of the screen, there are two different page tab options: Followers and Direct.

By default, Instagram takes you to the '**Followers tab**' after you've selected your photo or video. If you want to send a post to one or more people privately, rather than posting it publicly, through Instagram Direct, use the Instagram Direct tab.

5. Choose Up to 15 Instagram Direct Recipients

The **Direct tab** allows you to type in a caption for your photo or video at the top. The list of users that you interact with the most on Instagram will populate first, then the rest of the users you follow. Scroll down and tap the circle to the right of each user's avatar, a green check mark appears, which selects them to be a recipient of your private Instagram message.

6. Watch Your Recipients Interact in Real-time

Once you send a message, Instagram will bring you to your inbox. A list of your most recent sent and received messages is found in your inbox.Tapping a recently sent message allows you to watch as recipients view it, like it or add a comment on it.

As recipients interact, their avatars appear below the photo or video. A green checkmark symbol appears if the recipient opened it, a red heart if they liked it,or a blue comment bubble if they wrote something in the comment section.

Bear in mind, when you select more than one person as a recipient for your message, everybody who receives it will be able to see all the interactions on it. This includes those who have viewed it, liked it, and commented on it. Anyone can add a comment below the photo or video to interact, or they may choose to tap the Reply button to send an entirely new photo or video message as response.

All of your Instagram Direct messages can be accessed at any time. Navigate to the home feed and tap the little **mailbox icon** in the top right corner. This is a great new option for group messaging and adds a nice touch to a growing mobile social network, allowing users to get more personal with our followers.

HOW TO USE INSTAGRAM FOR BUSINESS: A BEGINNER'S GUIDE

1. Create your Instagram strategy

Start off by doing some research. Use Instagram yourself, before using it for your brand. Check out the best businesses on Instagram and other brands in your industry, including your competitors, both for inspiration and competitive intelligence.

Once you're familiar with the app, begin to build your Instagram strategy. This strategy should mirror the broad social media marketing plan, which acts as your business' guide for social media activities.

First, establish your Instagram goals. These goals should tie back to your business goals. They might include:

- Increasing product sales
- Increasing traffic to your website
- Increasing brand awareness
- Increasing branded hash tag mentions

The goals you set for your Instagram strategy should all be achievable and measurable. For example, don't set a goal to increase your white paper downloads, if your Instagram activities can't be tied to your white papers. Hint: this would be difficult and probably wouldn't work. By creating goals that are measurable, you can track your progress.

Once you identify your goals, craft a mission statement for your Instagram account. A mission statement acts as a guiding principle for your Instagram activities, and will dissuade you from treating the social network like you would Twitter or Facebook. Specific features of each social media network lend themselves to certain goals. In the case of Instagram, the network's power is in visuals, and your mission statement and goals should reflect that. The statement will likely take on format similar to:

We will use Instagram for (purpose of this social network) in order to help (business goal).

With your mission statement at hand, you can move onto your content strategy. This involves:

- Deciding how often to post
- Choosing what time of the day to post
- Establishing a content calendar
- Choosing your content themes

On Instagram, maintain regular posting schedules, but don't bombard your followers with too many posts. Most brands release one to three posts per day. As for what time of day to post, this largely depends on your audience. For both of these factors, frequency and time, it comes down to testing. Test posts at different intervals and times and see what works best. This will depend on the location of your audience, including their timezone, among other factors. Use that insight to establish a content calendar. Your calendar should establish who is in charge of posting, when they'll post, and what the content willbe.

With Hootsuite's new Instagram integration, Instagram posts can be scheduled in advance. This allows you to save time on posting every day, allowing you to dedicate more of your resources to engagement and community building. Spend a bit of time each week scheduling your Instagram images at your audience's most active times and check back in as necessary.

Choosing the themes and subject matter for your content is a big deal on Instagram, so I'll go into it in more detail:

2. Build your Instagram brand

Instagram is all about the visuals. Set out to build a cohesive, recognizable brand identity. How you approach your Instagram brand will be influenced by the strategy you have determined.

Consider the visual style you want for your Instagram brand. Choose one filter or a set of filters to use for the majority, if not all your photos.

By using the same filters, you establish a style that will become recognizable to your followers. Your goal is to get Instagram users to stop scrolling once they see your image, in order to engage with it by liking or commenting. Therefore, the more instantly recognizable your photos are, the better.

Take a look at 33 Acres Brewing Company. This company's Instagram uses white borders and a very white colour pallet in the majority of their photos. Scrolling through their feed, the style quickly becomes familiar and you start to associate images that meet these characteristics with the brewery.

Other mobile photo editing apps like VSCOcam and Whitagram can provide additional filters or editing options to help you find a style. Photos that have been edited or filtered elsewhere can also be imported into Instagram.

Decide what content your photos will focus on. In some cases, the content will be obvious: a clothing line will shoot photos of clothes; a restaurant will shoot photos of its food. Not all industries have this luxury. Brands from all industries are finding ways to promote themselves through lifestyle content, which seems to connect well with the Instagram audience. You don't have to be a lifestyle brand to post lifestyle content. Hootsuite is a social media management company. In my company, we share Instagram photos of our staff members, dogs and offices. We share content that represents the character and culture of our business.

If unsure of how to visually represent your own company, monitor the accounts of your followers. Look at what they're sharing and see if you can identify any trends, then replicate the visual themes in your own content.

An accounting firm might find their followers are very passionate about coffee or cars, and share content from their employees which fits these themes. Also, brands could share their followers' photos, giving them full credit of course, as a form of user-generated content. The marker company, Sharpie, uses UGC regularly in their feed, interspersing it with product photos to great effect. The use of UGC and lifestyle content makes the product shorts feel less obtrusive and salesy, as a result.

Finally, there are non-visual elements to your Instagram brand, like common language or style for captions. A popular technique used by brands is the branded hashtag. This doesn't mean using your company name as a hashtag. Instead, find a hashtag that embodies your Instagram brand and encourages followers to share photos that fit that image. Brands receive the benefit of increased exposure to new potential customers. Instagram users participate for a chance to be featured on a brand's profile, as prestige and an increase in followers comes along with it.

Manage Several Accounts

The latest version of Instagram will allow you to monitor five accounts at the same time. Many digital marketers are familiar with switching from one account to another. Probably, you have experienced managing both your personal and business account. Thanks to the latest addition, you can now save time, and you can also add likes to the posts from your other profiles. In order to enable this feature, just search your setting, and choose the Add Account feature, then add the profiles that you like to manage. Once you are ready to switch between profiles, just hold your finger above the icon on the bottom right of the screen and wait until a pop up menu appears to allow you to switch between your added profiles.

Aim to Be Featured by Other Instagram Users

Basically, there are two ways to be featured by other Instagram users: First, tag the brands with photos that showcase you using their products, and second, develop content like a creative work to honor the influencer or the brand. The ideal strategy for these tactics is to develop high-quality images that could either showcase their brand in an interesting or positive light. In posting, just make certain to tag their official account, so they will notice. However, you should use this tactic sparingly as your brand should not be known for passing on the limelight to other brands. Aim to find your own voice and resonate it by building your own brand.

Top Tools Essential for Instagram Marketing

With a social media calendar for Instagram can help you plan ahead your posts, you can use available tools to improve your marketing strategy. I have decided to list here my favorite Instagram tools so it will be easier for you. Evaluate your present strategy, assess the behavior of your target audience, and develop posts that will help your audience engage with your brand. Choose the best tools according to your brand and your goals and be familiar with them so you can achieve optimal results.

Hootsuite

Hootsuite is an online tool that makes social media management easy and efficient. This platform can help you schedule and post content on Facebook, Twitter, Pinterest, and of course, Instagram. You can use Hootsuite's Instagram option for scheduling your content in advance, so you don't have to worry about publishing on the right time. After preparing your content for publishing, you can now manage your other concerns for your brand marketing. Once the posting comes, Hootsuite will notify you. Remember, Instagram does not allow external apps to publish directly so you have to post them yourself. Other similar platforms are Buffer and Crowdfire.

SocialRank

SocialRank is another helpful Instagram tool, which provides you the opportunity to assess the insight into the demographics of your followers. You can also manage, identify, and organize your followers. When the tool has gained the profiles of your followers, you can then filter and group them based on different categories. Then, you can easily export the lists of your followers and use them for your own evaluation. This social media tool is ideal for gathering data about your followers' age, location, and gender. However, you can also figure out other important factors to determine what your followers want and adjust your strategies and tactics accordingly. Remember, knowing your audience is a factor for starting your Instagram marketing. This tool is an excellent companion to get to know your audience.

Instagram Feed WD

Instagram Feed WD is a plugin that you can use to bring your hashtag-based feeds to your own website with only several clicks or taps. You can access a composite feed of users and hashtags using a custom style and imaging. The tool allows you to use visually appealing layouts such as Blog Style, Masonry, Browser, or thumbnail. The plugin can be used to show the filtered feeds, which you can base on the specific username, mention, hashtag, media link or description. Other features of Instagram Feed WD includes sorting by categories, mixed and multiple feeds, social sharing buttons, widget, advanced lightbox, customizable themes, Instagram comments, and SEO friendly.

Boomerang

Boomerang is a great tool that can help you for creating videos, which will appeal to your audience. The unique feature of Boomerang is that you can film videos that are only one second long. The best thing about the video produced using Boomerang is that there is that there is no need for too much preparation because the videos don't have any audio. Hence, there is no need to work on the dialogues or your script. You just need to capture the best moment behind the scenes or make an interesting video about your product or service. This is a creative way to drive engagement for your brand.

Crowdfire

Crowdfire is a tool that you can use to manage your Instagram followers. This tool can identify people who are not following you or who has been inactive for several months. The tool provides daily prescription to grow your profile. Crowdfire will also prompt you quickly to begin following users who may be interested in your product or service. It provides the suggestions about who you can follow by depending on your following behaviors. Moreover, you could use the tool for keeping track of the effects of your updates on the followers.

Foursixty

While you may use Instagram mainly for brand awareness, you can use this platform to add more revenue to your business. With Foursixty, you can sell your products on Instagram by connecting your content to your product page. Also, your followers will have the chance to add items to your carts rather than taking extra effort to browse the web for your website. Another tactic that you can use is to post customer testimonials on Instagram as it is an indication to your followers that you are a reliable brand. With this tool, you can enable Instagram to encourage your followers to buy your products and so convert them into actual paying customers.

VSCO

Because Instagram is mainly for the visual senses, ensure to add VSCO into your marketing mix. VSCO is a great tool for capturing and editing images. It can help you manage the visual aspect of your marketing strategy. You can use different filters to tailor-fit your images and make them more appealing for your audience. You can capture images of your products or take spectacular scenery, which can be a good theme for your marketing campaigns. Based on recent statistics from Social Media Sprout, there are about 80 million photos shared on Instagram every day. For your brand to stand out, your content should be more than just great photos. Look for a theme, which will be constant in the images that promote your products and use VSCO to make them great.

Repost

Repost is a remarkable tool that you can use to share user-generated content. With this, you can show your customers that you are appreciating them as well as their posts. It is easy to use Repost, as you just need to click and share that post that you want to share, while tagging the original source of the post. Using Repost, you can bookmark any content on Instagram that you want to share to your audience. You can also search for pictures that you like by searching for a specific hashtag or the handle of a specific follower and repost content by tapping one button. Repost can help you nurture the relationship you are building with your audience.

Social Insight

Social Insight is a tool that you can use on Instagram to run a comprehensive analysis of your account. You can keep track of your account growth, engagement and interaction. The primary feature of this tool will allow you to estimate the best time for sharing content and gain data on your audience. You could also see the data on your average engagement. Moreover, if you are managing several brands on Instagram, this tool will allow you to link all of them and do a comparison of the analytics. This is among the best Instagram tools that you can use for marketing your brand.

Instagram Business Blog

Instagram has recently launched their Business Blog, which will serve as a hub for business owners to learn more on how they can use Instagram for their marketing campaigns. As a marketer or business owner, you should make certain to visit the blog regularly to be updated on the latest trends on Instagram and how you can use the available tools effectively. According to statistics released by Instagram, almost 49% of brands have their own Instagram account, which includes 90% of the top 100 global brands. This shows that the competition is getting stiffer, and you have to use each tool to make sure that you stay ahead of the game.

Facebook Power Editor

Because Instagram is owned by Facebook, you need to use Facebook Power Editor to generate sponsored content. When you use this tool, you can easily target factors of your audience that you want to see your ads such as location, age, gender, habits or interest. This tool can help you develop ads on Instagram that are more likely to be received well by your customers. The good thing is, you don't need to shell out thousands of dollars to reach out to your customers. Even a $1 budget per day is enough as long as you have identified your audience. Of course, if you want to reach more people, you have to invest more in your sponsored content.

Instagram has the potential to become among the most powerful business platforms online if you use it with the right tools and the right strategy and tactics. There are many tools available and you should not hesitate to try them. Look for the tools that you think can help you achieve your goals and begin improving your content strategy and tactics on daily posting.

CHAPTER SIX:
YOUTUBE

YouTube is a video sharing and hosting website that allows users to post and distribute their own videos online. Anyone with a camcorder can make a video and broadcast it on YouTube, to a vast audience of hundreds of millions of users. YouTube is the largest provider of online video in the world and has 44% of the world's market share for online video. According to the CEO of YouTube, there are more than 4 billion video views every day, which gives perspective of how many people are watching free online videos. A lot more than are watching the local TV station!

YouTube is the fourth most visited website on the planet, after Google, Facebook and Yahoo. YouTube is a phenomenon that cannot afford to be ignored, for marketing purposes.

Getting started on YouTube is easy. Establish an account using your Google Gmail address, if you have one, or establish a new user ID for free. Once establishing your ID, setup your profile and customize your home page. Just like with Facebook and the other social networking sites, add your photo, bio, along with contact information, and links back to your website. YouTube also allows users to add a blog, which is a great feature. Every time a video is uploaded to YouTube, it can be automatically posted to your blog(s). Now that your account is established, start uploading videos.

Your account is sub divided into videos, channels and shows. You can choose to subscribe to other users' videos and users will often subscribe back to yours. It is important to stick to your theme or business. If involved in real estate, one would subscribe to real estate related videos. Don't subscribe to non-business related videos. Setup a different personal YouTube account for that.

Large national chains are using YouTube to effectively promote their products and services.

Here is an example of Home Depot and how they are using YouTube:

http://www.youtube.com/user/HomeDepot.

Here is another example from University of Phoenix Online:

http://www.youtube.com/user/UniversityofPhoenix.

What do these companies know about online marketing that many other companies do not? They know that there are 800 million unique visitors on YouTube every month. These visitors can watch online videos for free. These companies also know how to effectively market and sell their product or service to these users. They figured out that if it is worthwhile to produce commercials for TV, it is more worthwhile to produce them for online video channels like YouTube.

The YouTube audience is larger and global. The production of online video is now part of an advertising budget in large companies. These companies understand social networking, its impact on business, and understand how important online marketing is. So, how can you employ YouTube to your advantage? YouTube can be a very effective way to make cheap infomercials about your products or services. These videos can be posted on YouTube and the content from these videos can be utilized on web sites and capture pages.

Every video on YouTube has an embed feature which allows any other user (not just the person that uploaded the video) to embed the content of the video in to their website. If you could make a video that other people find useful, then they would embed that video into their own website. You can also choose to embed the video into your own website.

YouTube is owned by Google and as mentioned before, it is free. This fact is very important because the search engines index the videos on YouTube based on their descriptions. Each video has tags which

116

are keywords related to the content of that particular video. For example, if I post a video about wholesaling bank owned properties, then I might add the following tags: "wholesaling, real estate, bank owned properties, Miami Mansion, wholesale, flip and fliphouses"

These tags will be attributed to that specific video only and indexed by the search engines. If you look on Google's home page, there is a video link to search for videos online. Since Google owns YouTube, the search engine gives preference to YouTube videos. If your video is about a topic related to the search, it will show up in the search rankings. Tags from that video help Google identify what the video is about. Always add as many relevant tags as possible to every video that is uploaded for maximum exposure.

Also, be sure that the description for each video is completed with many keywords related to the content of the video. A link back to your website can be useful.

It is very important to create a catchy title. I have found that I get a lot more hits on a video, when the title is a little scandalous. If on the above video example, I called the title, "I made $30,000 without even trying", then that video would get more hits. The more important question is: what will these users do once they get to the video? Will they visit my site or just click back? The more relevant your topic, your description, and your tag words the more likely that they will go to your site. Once again, make it easy for people to follow you online and connect with you, have links to your website, how to contact you, etc.

Using videos for capture pages is a great way to drive traffic. If a video has some good content that gets good viewer counts it can become viral (spread around the internet) very quickly.

Start thinking about what you could do to create a video that would be of interest to others. If the video is funny, then that is sometimes a good way to make a video go viral. Don't make just one video. Make a point of constantly uploading new videos about your product or service. Then use this video to embed in your website and on your capture pages. Post links to the videos on Facebook and Twitter.

The video does not necessarily have be high quality. For example, if you type in the words "Learn How TO Wholesale Real Estate" into YouTube, a few of my videos will come up.

If you end up shooting videos, uploading them to YouTube and then directing traffic back to your website will increase traffic dramatically. The more creative your video, keywords and concept, the more likely you are to get more hits. Remember that it isn't necessary to spend money on professional production quality videos. Provide relevant, informative, educational topics that are timely and of interest to your target audience. Add YouTube to your marketing toolbox and watch your traffic to your web site grow exponentially.

CHAPTER SEVEN: TWITTER

Twitter is a very popular social media site and app that began in 2006. It is one of the fastest growing social networking services in the world. It registers over 250 million unique visitors per month. That means 250 million people that have never been to the Twitter website before, visit it in just one month. The number of registered users on Twitter has grown at a rate faster than almost any other website on the planet surpassing even Facebook in the number of new users signed up (in the first few years).

Twitter is a free social networking and micro blogging platform. Users send "tweets" which are text-based messages, which are no more than 140 characters long. These messages or tweets can be sent via mobile texting, instant message, or the web. Anyone can log on to Twitter and register for free. The important thing to know is that once you register, your username will be visible to everyone. You might want to think before choosing a username. We discussed this concept on the chapter about branding.

The user name shows like this: *twitter.com/username,* so continuing with the previous example, *www.Twitter.com/MiamiMansion,* would be a good username. If not branding your business name, then you should be branding your own name as we mentioned in the branding chapter.

Once you have registered, the next thing to do is to upload your profile picture. Then upload your short bio (no more than 160 characters) and choose a background under settings. Choose the settings tab to add your website and verify your username and bio for your profile. If you want to customize your profile further, you can use a company like twit art, *http://twitart.com*, to further customize your profile. If customizing your background image, it is a good idea to put your photo and logo. Include your contact information as well, such as telephone number, email address and website. Adding social bookmarking sites like Facebook, Linked-in and YouTube to your Twitter background will make it easier for people to connect with you online. You can see an example of a customized twitter background by looking at my twitter profile.

Now that you are on Twitter, you're ready to begin "following" people. Choose people that are in your industry and type in keywords to find other Twitter users that you can follow. For example, if you are in the real estate industry, type in "real estate" and see Twitter users that have the word "real estate" in their user name or their bio. The rule of thumb on Twitter is that when someone follows you, be polite and follow them back. The only exception is if their profile picture or brand is not something that you would want to be associated with. Then simply ignore them and do not follow back.

The more people you follow in your field, the more people will follow you back. There are quite a few celebrities on Twitter for example Oprah, Shaq, Al Gore, Ben Stiller, Arnold Schwarzenegger and hundreds of others. For starters, choose to follow some of these people if you wish and then look for people in your industry or people that you know. Many more people and companies are now advertising their Twitter profile on their company websites, and in email correspondence.

Now that you're online and have some followers, you are ready to begin "tweeting". This is the part that everyone does not understand about Twitter. Anyone can tweet anything, so some people tweet insignificant things such as what they ate for lunch or what they are doing right now (which is of no particular interest to anyone). However, Twitter is much more than this. Please do not make the mistake of briefly looking at Twitter and then moving on. Most Twitter users follow less than 100 people. They briefly look at Twitter, don't understand what the big deal is and then lose interest.

Every single "tweet" is posted online which means that it is indexed by the search engines like Google, Yahoo, and MSN. (There is currently a dispute between Google and Twitter which has temporarily restricted tweets from being indexed but this is supposed to be resolved soon). Tweets being indexed means that someone typing in a keyword on a Google search could potentially stumble on to your Twitter profile. Is this a good thing? Well it is if you have a link to your website or capture page from that tweet. If they click on your website, you have now diverted traffic from a search engine to your website for free. And if you "capture" their information, that is even better.

Search engines like new information. For example, a website is static and does not change day to day. Tweets are dynamic. They are changing everyday, so they are given a higher priority on search engines because the information is fresh. This is what makes Twitter so powerful. You could hire someone to tweet the same thing but in different words using keywords that Google itself tells you are relevant. This same person that you pay could also click and follow all day long for you. You could turn your Twitter account into a huge search engine optimization tool for almost no money. This is what big companies are now doing. They are actually hiring people to tweet.

Other creative ways that you can use Twitter are to hold sweep stakes and issue discount coupons. For example, you could have a sweepstake that says everyone that follows you on Twitter will be entered into a drawing tow in a free prize. People that re-tweet (tell other Twitter users about your tweet) get additional votes for re-tweets. You have now given people a financial incentive to follow you and to distribute (retweet) your tweets to other users. Do you think that could be useful?

Creative ways of using Twitter for business are popping up every day. Using Twitter for business is still relatively new. This concept of promotions and sweepstakes on Twitter is still very underutilized by most business. However, some businesses use it very effectively. Another creative way to use twitter is to issue discount coupons. Your business can offer a free service to one lucky winner or you can simply offer a 10% discount to anyone that clicks on a link to redeem the coupon, which should be for a limited time only to induce a call to action. If you want to learn more about how to use Twitter for advertising campaigns, then Google the words Twitter and contest or giveaway and find out more information online. This is a rapidly evolving field and there are many new players entering it every day.

Remember that every new follower that you get on Twitter is another individual that you could be prospecting or marketing to. The easiest way to get many followers is to follow other people. The key though is to make sure that you are not just randomly following people but are instead following people in your niche. If you are in real estate, then use the "find people "search tool on Twitter to find people with the word "real estate" in their profile. This would be an example of targeted following.

You should use more than just one search keyword. For example, in my niche I would use words like foreclosure, short sale, Miami, real estate, etc. in order to find individuals that are on Twitter and have those words in their profile. There are other ways to find targeted followers. One of the easiest is to simply follow people that are following other people. The best way to do this is to see what your competitors and business associates are doing in your industry. Look up key people in your industry on Twitter and start following their followers. Since their followers are interested in what they have to say, and your message is similar; the theory is that they will be interested in what you have to say too.

While we are on the topic of interesting things to say, make sure that you are contributing something interesting when you tweet. It is okay to solicit a service or product that you have to sell but you should make sure that your followers are only hearing about it no more than 10% of the time. For every 10 tweets that you make, only one should have a product or service that you are trying to sell. The rest should be informational or educational, motivating or interesting. What kinds of things can you tweet about?

Here are a few ideas:

- Motivational quotes that motivate others and you are always positive and uplifting which makes people want to follow you

- Interesting news topics and newspaper or magazine articles related to your industry which your followers might be interested in

- Breaking news that is somehow related to your industry — search Google news for this

- Links to videos or websites that are related to your industry and your followers might find interesting

- Anything that can be re-tweeted that was written by others but that is interesting to your followers

If you follow many people, eventually you will reach the 2,000 follow limit. This is not really a limit since you can follow as many people as you want. However, once you reach the limit of following 2,000 people, Twitter wants to make sure that people are following you back before it lets you follow more people. So, you need to un-follow people that do not follow you. However, you need to be very careful not to do this over short periods of time. If you do, then Twitter might shut your account down.

I suggest that you do a targeted follow and then wait a week or so to give people the opportunity to follow you back. If after a week they still have not followed you back, then they either are not interested in following you or they don't have the time or inclination to log onto Twitter to follow back. After a week has passed you can un-follow those people that are not following you back. Why would you want to do this? Because after you are following 2,000 people, Twitter will only let you follow up to 10% of your followers (up to 2,200 people). Therefore, the only way for you to follow more people is to get more people to follow you. The only way that you can do this is to constantly un-follow those that are not following you back. For a graphic depiction of who you are following that is not following you back visit *http://www.friendorfollow.com.*

There are many different software programs and websites that can automate this and many other Twitter tasks. Most of them violate Twitter's terms of service so I do not encourage you to use these programs. Many companies hire virtual assistants or social media coordinators that charge a monthly fee to handle these procedures for business. This fact alone should give you pause to consider whether or not Twitter is a useful business application. Why would large corporate companies be employing social marketing directors and employees whose sole task is to log on and monitor their social networking sites like Twitter?

For an example of this that we mentioned before take a look at *http://www.dell.com/twitter* to see how large corporate companies are using Twitter. Notice too how they have customized their Twitter link.

I have a compiled a list of other useful web sites that complement Twitter and are worthy of mentioning. Please note that there are so many new sites popping up all of the time that keeping this list current is a challenge. I am listing only a few of the tools that have been around for a few years. There are many others if available online with more being added daily. Google Twitter Tools to see the latest.

Social Oomph

This popular website will definitely give your Twitter account some oomph. Social oomph has some very useful features which you can use to make your Twitter account more efficient. Social Oomph allows you to bulk schedule tweets ahead of time. You could schedule famous quotes (which are great to tweet) to go out each morning and you could have it scheduled ahead of time. Another useful feature is the auto follow feature which works very well.

But the most useful feature by far is the auto direct message. When someone follows you on Twitter, you have the option of sending them a message that says something like "thanks for following me". This is what most people do. However, efficient marketers do something much better than this. They set up a direct message that brings users to a capture page or product page. The key is to do this in such a way that it is not interpreted as selling or spam. Do send people to a page for access to a free report. It is acceptable practice to ask for their email address in order to deliver them the report. Now that you have done that you have the option of adding them to your data base. As long as it is easy for them to unsubscribe, then you should not have any problems.

But please don't spam people with irrelevant information. And whatever you do with your direct message on Twitter DO NOT send them to a page that asks them to buy something. That is the easiest way to insult them and they will definitely not follow you. Here is the website link for Social Oomph: *http://www.socialoomph.com*

Nearby Tweets

The unique feature I like is the fact that it registers the geographic location of other Twitter users. It also allows a keyword search. You can log on to this site and it will show you geographically based on however many miles designated, who is on Twitter in your area. The really amazing feature is when you combine this with a key word. For example, if I type in real estate and a geographic location of 50 miles, I can see who has the word "real estate" in their profile or who tweets about real estate. And I can then target this Twitter audience to people that are within a certain distance of my location. This is a unique feature for allowing people to know about meetings, events etc., that are limited to a specific geographic location that is local to them that they might be interested in. For example, if I were to post a real estate networking event on Twitter, these individuals may be interested in attending the event. If they come to the event, I then have the opportunity to monetize that traffic by capturing their name and email address when they attend the meeting. Information can be capture online and offline. The key is for that information to be stored in a database. Here is the link for this website: *http://www.nearbytweets.com*

Tweet Deck

Tweet Deck is a free desktop application that you can download and install on your computer. It basically breaks down all tweets, replies to tweets and direct messages. This makes it easier to follow a conversation on Twitter. It also makes it really easy to re-tweet something. Tweet Deck also allows you to group your friends and create keyword groups. The software takes a while to get used to, but the application is extremely useful.

http://www.tweetdeck.com

Topsy.com

If you are looking for something interesting to tweet, then you should visit this website *http://www.topsy.com*. Think of it as the Google search engine of tweets. It shows the most popular tweets, along with keywords and topics that are the most popular. This service is very useful to find out fast what is relevant in news and any topic including the real estate industry. The search engines are now ranking tweets too. As I mentioned previously Google, Yahoo and Bing are now indexing all tweets which can drive traffic to your website. TV and news reporters now monitor real time sites like topsy.com, to see where breaking news is coming from.

Multiple Profiles on Twitter

Many twitter users are unaware that Twitter allows users to have multiple profiles. You should use a different email address to register a different profile in order to keep track of everything. However, your different profile needs to be for a specific reason. Twitter does not allow you to simply have multiple profiles. For example, I have a profile for my cheap houses' website, a profile for my real estate investment club, and a profile for my main website.

Why might an additional profile be useful? The answer is more eyeballs. More traffic equals more revenue. You should have at least one Twitter profile for yourself and one for your company.

Having multiple Twitter profiles allows you to leverage your exposure to many more people. Using the six degrees of separation concept, think of how many more people would see your posts if you had two profiles with thousands of followers instead of just one. You can separate your Twitter profiles to distinguish them apart from each other. For example, you could set up a Twitter profile specifically for a product that you sell or a service that you provide.

Twitter snobs are people that allow others to follow them and do not follow back. Unless the individual is a famous celebrity, stop following these people since they will distort your ratio of following to followers once you reach the 2,000 limits.

And if you think following 2,000 people is a lot, try following 50 people a day and it will take you only 40 days to follow 2,000 people. Remember that social networking should be part of your marketing and advertising budget and is definitely worthy of your time. Just make sure that you monitor your time and don't get carried away. The best plan is to allocate a set time per day for social networking. If you set aside 30 to 60 minutes per day and make it part of your routine it will become a habit after a few weeks.

You can also establish third party applications that work together with Twitter. For example, Facebook, Flickr, You Tube, Linked-In, Meetup and many other social networking sites have applications that work with Twitter. Every time you tweet something it can show upon your profile on all of these sites. This is very beneficial because it lets everyone that follows or is friendly with you become more aware of you and your business. It is also very beneficial because each one of these tweets will show up in the search engines, which will help drive targeted traffic to your website or capture page. Keep this in mind when you are tweeting and keep your focus on your topic, your business and your industry.

Custom URL Links

Since Twitter limits your message to 140 characters, you will find yourself constantly trying to shorten your message. This is a good thing since you should always try and deliver a clear and concise message using as few words as possible. In the words of Mark Twain "use plain, simple language, short words and brief sentences."

Your readers will be bored easily, and they will just skim over your tweet in less than a second. For this reason, make sure that you are expressing relevant words immediately instead of filling up the 140-character limit. Also make sure that the important points are at the beginning and not at the end of the 140 characters. Don't feel obligated to use all of the characters either.

You will find it quite challenging to convey your message in 140 characters or less and for this reason, custom URL links are a good idea. There are a few URL shortening services but I will primarily discuss the two main URL shortening web sites which are *http://www.tinyurl.com* and *http://www.bit.ly*. Custom URL shortening sites allow you to shorten or customize your link.

CHAPTER EIGHT: LINKEDIN

Linkedln is more old school than Facebook. Traditionally Linkedln was the social networking site of choice for older users who were looking for a professional place to network online with other users in the workplace. Many of these users used Linkedln as a way to have their resume online and keep themselves in front of potential employers. Employers and recruiters in turn used Linkedln to find new employees.

There are two main reasons why Linkedln is perfect for real estate agents and brokers:

Linkedln is More Effective Than Twitter and Facebook for Lead Generation

Linkedln is 227% more effective regarding lead generation than Twitter and Facebook according to a recent HubSpot study. While there are more users and activity on the other two social media sites, those platforms are mostly tailored towards advertising and making friends, instead of building a professional network.

However, you can still link your advertisements on Twitter and Facebook to your Linkedln profile as part of a wholesome lead generation strategy.

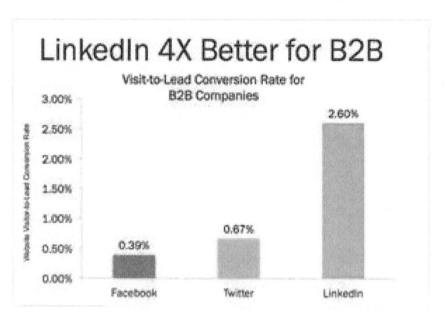

LinkedIn 4X Better for B2B

Visit-to-Lead Conversion Rate for B2B Companies

Customers Use LinkedIn to Learn From, Vet And Network With Agents

When it comes to marketing, a laser-focused audience is better than a broader, more diverse audience. This is why I propose that you buy ads on Zillow through Zillow Premier Agent.

While Facebook ads will expose your brand to a larger number of people, almost every user on the Zillow platform is there to perform a real estate purchase or sale. This means that traffic to your LinkedIn content via Zillow will be streamlined to your target audience compared to a more social platform.

While many people do not view LinkedIn as a platform to find a real estate agent or check listings, they usually visit LinkedIn to learn and network with other professionals. This is the secret reason England LinkedIn real estate marketing is an awesome way to engage prospects and leads when they are most interested in learning about your services and networking within the real estate community.

If you post good content on your LinkedIn profile, prospects will view your brand as more professional and hirable.

LinkedIn Networking For Realtors

To increase your real estate leads on LinkedIn, you need to learn the basic principles that influence networking. Your employees and colleagues that follow you are first degree connections while others are ranked as a second degree or third degree depending on your level of interaction. You can grow your network by linking second-degree connections with the InMail feature to broaden your reach. Unlike Twitter and Facebook that allows you to follow or add almost anyone, LinkedIn restricts networking options based on the strength of your connection. As a Realtor on LinkedIn, your goal should be to get as many local connections as you can within a short amount of time, hence, understanding the intricacies of LinkedIn connections is a vital skill to possess.

3 Steps to Creating a Powerful Email Marketing Campaign Through LinkedIn

Let's create a scenario where you are at a networking event, and you spot someone you don't know but want to link with. Maybe she is one of the most successful realtors in your area, and you would like to model your business after theirs, or a potential joint venture partner.

How would you approach this person? Would you walk up to them and sweet talk them into promoting your business, or request for his or her time? Chances are, they won't fulfill your request because there is no existing relationship between you and the person.

The same logic applies to LinkedIn, and I often witness many people making the same mistake of pitching their service to me immediately I connect with them. This feels of laziness and is not professional. Desperate tactics like these are unlikely to elicit the right response from people you want to connect with.

It might seem like common sense, but you cannot begin to imagine the number of people that squander golden opportunities by sending generic automated messages that make it easy to be ignored. Actions like this have the potential to burn the relationship want to cultivate, and even have them report to LinkedIn to sever any connection with you.

In the world of business, there are no shortcuts to marketing success, so before you start pitching your real estate services to anyone, you need to cultivate a healthy business relationship with them, build customer trust, and show why you are an expert in your industry.

One of the most amazing things about LinkedIn is the ability to connect privately with nearly anyone on the planet and then dive into the email market once you have networked with the right audience. If properly executed, LinkedIn affords you the opportunity to get your real estate services in front of hundreds if not thousands of important decision-makers in the real estate industry every month.

If we are keeping it a buck, compared to other social media platforms, LinkedIn offers more expressive capabilities.

Below, I have provided a 3-step process to creating an engaging marketing campaign through LinkedIn so that you can convert your connections to leads and sales for your real estate business.

1. Segment Your Contacts

In the marketing world, it has become increasingly important to link up with your customer effectively. The key term to focus on is "relevance." It is important to note that the services you provide to someone in an executive role are going to differ significantly from someone in an intern role. What resonates with a category of your target audience might not work for another aspect.

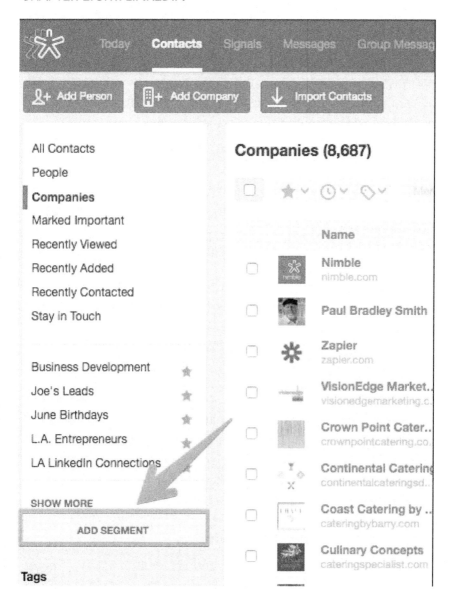

A lot of people do not realize that you can categorize your connections into topic segments within LinkedIn. The platform allows users to classify their connections by subject areas. This is referred to as "tagging" on the site.

Tagging allows you to organize your connections by subject or industry. This is a useful feature as it helps you to tailor your marketing messages to the most relevant networks that are specific to your members.

Before you send your next email, take a moment to segment your current contacts to make sure every content you send out is personalized and targeted to a specific audience.

2. Think About The Finish Line

Once the contacts have been segmented, the next step is designing your call to action. This is the process that covers the entirety of the sales funnel and details every step and action you want to guide your contacts through once you have cultivated a healthy business relationship with them.

This could be attending one of your webinars, downloading a whitepaper, a face-to-face meeting, or phone meeting. It depends on the prices of your service, company sales cycle, and target demographic.

A good example is Linkfluencer whose call to action is a free download of their E-book or LinkedIn webinar. As a real estate agent and realtor, your call to action can be a free consultation or E-book download of real estate books. This works well because it allows you to educate the target audience and explores the methodology on how they can get the best real estate deals and related tips.

3. The LinkedIn Email Marketing Campaign

After you have successfully segmented your contacts and created your call to action, the final step is to create an email marketing campaign where you provide relevant, targeted content to your connections through a series of emails that are tailored to promote your call to action. These emails should typically include:

- Sharing real estate business tips and strategy.
- Sharing relevant articles in the real estate industry.
- Links to your whitepaper.

The purpose of a call to action is to provide value before offering your services. It is just like dating! Provide value and interest the target person before showing your services. It's that simple.

With more than 562 million users, LinkedIn is focused on building connections and networks. This is not limited to your immediate connections. It also expands to who your connections know. This is the real power of LinkedIn. In business, the ability to key into existing connections and expand your brand through word-of-mouth is very important. This is why I believe it is the number one platform for lead generation.

If your LinkedIn marketing strategy is tied to your profile, it's time to step up your game. A detailed company page is required if you want to expand your audience and boost business results.

According to research data from Hootsuite, company pages that have been completed attract twice as many visitors compared to the ones with incomplete company pages. Organizations that post content on a monthly basis get followers six times faster than companies that don't post.

The image below covers the entire process and includes some of the highlighted tips discussed.

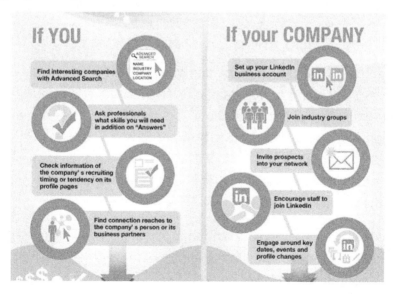

LinkedIn Company Page Is Essential

A company page provides LinkedIn members with the opportunity to learn about your brand, your business, and opportunities with your company. Company pages represent a great way to showcase industry expertise. A good example is Hootsuite's LinkedIn page that is followed by more than 190,000 people who regularly get content from the company. Your business can garner more exposure by providing valuable content for real estate industry powerhouses. LinkedIn Company pages act as HR landing pages for businesses.

Though this can be considered as the primary use of the platform, it is also the perfect network to raise brand awareness, drive business results, educate potential customers, and promote career opportunities. Engaging content and scintillating status updates will surely establish your brand as a frontrunner in your industry.

Here's how to create a LinkedIn page for your business

If you don't have a personal a LinkedIn profile now, you need to create one before setting up a company page. After creating your personal LinkedIn profile, follow the steps highlighted below to set

Add Your Company

Navigate to the LinkedIn Marketing solutions gateway to creating a company page and to the blue "Create a company page" button. Input your official business name and pick a URL that will allow potential leads and prospects to find your business on the platform. The URL cannot be changed, so it is wise to pick a standard one. Tick the confirmation box that you are acting on behalf of your brand, and then select Create Page.

LinkedIn immediately creates the shell of the company page. All that is required is for you to fill in the appropriate details. Navigate back to the pop-up box and click on Get Started.

Add a Cover Image and Logo

Select a cover image that captures the theme of your brand. Ideally, the image resolution should be 1536 × 768 pixels. Since LinkedIn is a professional platform, the logo represents the profile picture on other social platforms. The logo will also appear on the LinkedIn profiles of your employees. Make sure the logo is a pure image and at a resolution of east 300 × 300 pixels.

Do not skip this important step. LinkedIn data proves that brands with logos attract six times more engagement to their company pages.

Create a Company Description

Describe your real estate company does in 2000 characters and explain why potential followers should interact with you. This text is very important, so get your content and marketing team involved the process of crafting your company description. The first 156 characters appear in Google preview of your company page and must be treated critically. Below the company description, you can add as many as 20 company specialties. These specialties act as keyword and pointers to help other users find your business on the LinkedIn network. Ensure that your company's services and strengths are fully displayed in this section.

If you don't know what to write in this section, simply try some social listening to get a sense of what is trending in the industry online. This must be done from the customer's point of view.

Input Your Company Details

Fill in the URL for your website. After doing this, provide your company details via the drop-down menus to choose the company size, industry, company type (public, educational, non-profit, and so on), and the year your real estate business was founded. A physical location for your business must also be provided.

If you are already part of relevant LinkedIn groups that you want to add to your company page, simply add them to the appropriate section. Otherwise, leave the field blank.

Publish Your Page

Tap the Publish button to make your company page go live. Before performing any action, tap the Go To Member view button located on the top right corner of the page to see a preview of what your company page looks like. If the page is to your satisfaction, then proceed. If not, select Manage Page to make any required changes until you get it right.

Add Page Administrators

Even if you solely operate your business, you have the option to choose other users that can administer the page. To add team members, tap the Me icon at the top of the page and choose the Company Page option under the Manage section.

Select Admin Tools > Page Admins > Add team members by name. The other users that you have granted access to must be connected to you on LinkedIn before they can be page administrators. If you have any partners that are good with social marketing and the real estate industry, then they would make an excellent choice to manage the page.

Once you have successfully added other members to the company age, click on Save Changes to finish up.

Focus Solely On Continual Optimization

Now that you have successfully created your LinkedIn Company page, the next step is to ensure it is operating at its full potential. While creating a company page is relatively simple, don't let that trick you into proceeding without forming a solid LinkedIn business strategy to expand your page's benefits.

Instead of simply growing your connections and followers, you need to learn how to use LinkedIn marketing tools to identify me opportunities for growth.

Develop smart goals! You can never know how to achieve your goals if you do not clearly define the gold from the start. LinkedIn is a great platform to aid the growth of your real estate business, but you need to explicitly define what you want to derive from your LinkedIn profile. Are you trying to build a network for properties selling? Or establish yourself as a real estate mogul? Or host real estate seminars in your field?

If you want to diversify or focus on one aspect, you need to create goals and steps that will help you along the way, and then understand whether your efforts are lying of. Smart goals need to be measurable, specific, relevant, attainable, and time-bound.

Even if you are new to the world of LinkedIn business, you can access a lot of useful information vital for strategic planning and goal-setting by analyzing your connections and their medium of interactions across other social platforms.

Creating a company page won't automatically get you followers. However, I will provide proven business strategies and tips to boost your chances of success on the LinkedIn platform.

Get Your Employees To Connect With Your Company Page

The best way to grow an audience is by connecting with your colleagues and employees. LinkedIn data suggests that a strong company advocacy program is 58% more likely to attract engagement and 20% more likely to retain the following.

This is especially useful for first degree connections. By adding your employees and colleagues as followers, your company page will be linked to their profiles and vice versa.

Publish Engaging Content

One of the most creative ways to grow your audience on LinkedIn is to provide them with valuable content on a regular basis. I recommend at least one post per weekday. With the regular company updates appearing on your company page, they will simultaneously appear on your follower's news feeds.

If you are aware of any relevant articles or posts from an external source that can be beneficial to your followers, share the posts with them, even if the content isn't originally from your team, it shows that you are conversant with all the dealings in the real estate industry.

This will help boost connections with colleagues. Be sure to provide your insight on the shared content, instead of just copying and pasting the URL.

You can even try publishing thought pieces on the LinkedIn publishing network. Instead of just sharing content from other platforms to your website, a good way to boost your brand growth in the LinkedIn ecosystem is to create and publish content in-app. Even though articles cannot be published directly from the company page, the key personnel at your company can publish articles from their respective LinkedIn profiles to boost the presence of your brand on the platform.

Stand Out With Media Content

Granted, LinkedIn is a business-first network, but there are many ways to make your brand's content stand out from the norm. And one of such ways is to add images and videos to your posts. Generic text-only posts receive lesser engagement numbers compared to posts with media (a whopping 98% more comment).

You can also try to link videos from LinkedIn to your YouTube channel if you have one. Other social channels usually require users to upload videos remotely for auto play, on LinkedIn.

Use LinkedIn Groups

Being an active member of a LinkedIn group is beneficial to you and your business and is one of the best ways to network with other notable realtors and businesses in your field, especially outside of your immediate circle. Being an active participant in LinkedIn groups will attract engagement and views to your company page.

The first step is to find a group with similar interests and goals that align with your business model. Use the Search feature on your LinkedIn homepage or the Discover feature for groups. If you are up to it, create your real estate group. If you belong to any real estate associations, check to see if there's a LinkedIn group, as it can be a crucial source of networking and development.

When you join or create a group, you can add the group on your company page. To perform this action, tap the Me icon on your LinkedIn homepage > Choose your company page > select the Overview tab > scroll down to Featured groups > input the name of the group. Note that you can only add three groups to your company page.

Try Showcase Pages Feature

"Showcase Pages" works as a subdomain of the company page feature and allows users to highlight specific aspects of their business, like an ongoing initiative or a particular brand. Your followers on LinkedIn can choose to interact with your Spotlight pages if they want to understand a specific aspect of your brand.

It's particularly smart to segment your real estate business into categories like consultations, listings, white paper, properties, e-books, and other related parts of the brand.

Adobe brand, for example, has five Showcase Pages for five of its products that cater to different audiences.

Understand the LinkedIn Algorithm

While other social platforms like Facebook, Twitter, and Instagram keep their algorithm specifications secret, LinkedIn provides insight into how their network works. The LinkedIn algorithm works like this:

1. A bot analyzes your content as clear, low-quality, or spam. Hence quality is important if you are aiming for the top ranking.

2. LinkedIn algorithm measures user engagement and how they resonate with your followers. Are your posts attracting likes and comments? Awesome. Do your posts constantly get marked as spam? Not so awesome, after all. Quality is

key, and so is relevance. You need to make sure that your posts are useful to the real estate community.

3. The algorithm delves deeper into posts to crosscheck for credibility and spam based on the quality of your profile and your network.

4. Human editors review posted content to determine value. Relevant posts are disputed and even boosted.

Incorporate LinkedIn Ads

LinkedIn members provide the platform with information about their professional skills, interests, and associations. This infers that LinkedIn possesses extraordinary targeting capabilities that allow you to carry out laser-focused targeted decisions about integrating LinkedIn ads into your social media marketing strategy.

CHAPTER NINE:
SNAPCHAT MARKETING BASICS

When you look back on it, Snapchat has evolved from just being an ordinary app that lets users take, modify for fun, enjoy and share personal photos and videos to a formidable social media marketing platform. It used to be that snapping was limited to technologically-adept millennials but now, it's also very popular among social media marketers who are looking for fresh, new, and creative ways to tap new and exciting markets such as that of the millennials.

As mentioned earlier, Snapchat marketing may prove to be a bit formidable given the relatively short-lived nature of its contents. This means those who dare tread the exciting market of Snapchatters – and that includes you – need to be able to maximize the time they have on Snapchat. For this, certain basic strategies are crucial for successfully marketing your business on Snapchat.

Know Your Crowd

It's crucial to get a good grip on Snapchat's general crowd, even if your target audience isn't on the lower half of the age spectrum. What I mean is you'll have to understand that even if you're targeting executives for your marketing campaign, the general crowd or environment of Snapchat is very casual and rarely documents professional activities. It's not going to be in your best interests to use a formal or very corporate marketing strategy on Snapchat.

What does that look like? Generally speaking, this means your campaign or ads' tone of voice, one that'll be consistently applied to all your campaigns and must have a very casual, with a hint of fun, and must use words that are very easy to understand, instead

143

highly technical or corporate words and jargons. One tool you can use to achieve a relatively casual and fun feel to your campaigns is the app's drawing function, which can help your business appear more approachable and personable. Then your business will enjoy a much higher probability of successfully connecting with its target crowd or audience.

Considering you're relatively new to this platform, it'll be best not to rush into quickly launching a campaign but instead, take your time. Get to know your campaign's target crowds by simply browsing through other people's accounts and following other people so you can have a good grasp of Snapchat's best creative practices.

Accept Mortality

No, I'm not talking about yours. I'm talking about the relatively short life span of snapped photo and video contents on Snapchat, which is a mere 24-hours. While many inexperienced online marketers find this aspect of Snapchat to be more of a bane than a boon, experienced ones know how to use the short lifespan of the app's contents to stoke their target audiences' interest by teasing. The relatively short lifespan of Snapchat's content gives your target audience a sense of urgency to act quickly on your content before it's too late and the content's gone – that is if you play it right!

Another way to accept and even thrive on the mortality of Snapchat's contents is by conducting contests for your campaigns. For example, you can come up with a contest where users who snap pictures of themselves availing of your business's services, or patronizing its products are given freebies or prizes.

Generally speaking, the key to making the mortality factor of Snapchat's contents work for your campaigns' advantage is by consistently engaging your target crowd or audience. Doing so will give you even more opportunities to make them want more and keep coming back, which can only make it much easier for your marketing efforts to succeed.

Use Videos

While pictures do paint a thousand words, videos tell tens of thousands. Videos are simply more interesting and appealing. Videos speak more details about your business than photos. And the great thing about Snapchat is that content posted on the platform must be more casual than corporate or professional, which makes it easier for small business such as yours to come up with compelling video snaps for your campaigns.

Put Your Personality Forward

Social media marketing is all about engaging people, which require a certain level of personality. It's practically impossible to successfully conduct marketing campaigns on social media with a robotic or deadpan tone or approach. Having a persona or personality enables your business to connect with social media users. In short, you must "humanize" your business in your Snapchat and other social media campaigns.

When you snap videos and photos of your business, products and services, you must also post content that gives your target crowd an idea of the stuff that occurs behind the scenes. By letting everyone in your business contribute photos and videos of them doing their parts, it gives your target crowd the chance to become more intimate with your business and establish that all important connection.

Other Things to Consider

Many rookie Snapchat marketers are very careless with the things they snap. Don't be like one of them. Bad snaps on Snapchat have a tendency to be immortalized despite their short lifespan simply because its audience knows that snapped content will disappear within 24 hours and as such, they have a sense of urgency to save a screen shot of such content for sharing on other social media platforms, which don't delete content. So, think twice, or thrice, before you post something for your campaign. Even if you are very careful about the quality of the content you put out on Snapchat, your audience can also have too much of a good thing. As such, do not snap each and every movement or development in your business but only the best ones. Doing so is beneficial in two ways: it keeps your audiences wanting for more and it keeps your campaign from looking too excited or worse, desperate.

Snapchat is a very unique platform and as such, so are its contents. Therefore, avoid the temptation to share the same content you put out on your business' other social media accounts just for the sake of having something to post for your marketing campaign. Instead, use it to showcase other sides of your business that most people don't know about.

Timing is another very important aspect of a successful Snapchat marketing campaign. And by this, I mean the duration of the Snap's visibility. The default is 10 seconds, which can be too long for staring at a static photo. The best way to minimize this risk is to adjust our settings to a lower duration. Experiment with what seems to be the right amount of time to appreciate a snap.

Lastly, as much as Snapchat is a very cool social media platform for marketing your business, it's not the ideal place to post the really important stuff. In particular, don't share significant information or important announcements on Snapchat because of the short lifespan of contents posted on the platform. For the serious and important stuff, it's best to stick to other platforms that offer a great deal of content permanency. Snapchat is best for piquing the interest of your target audience by teasing them with limited content exposure about an upcoming product, service, or event.

CHAPTER TEN:
TUMBLR MARKETING

Tumblr is another primarily visual social media networking with an ever-increasing number of young users serving as its primary audience. You can include written works and articles on Tumblr, but it's ideal use is best suited to pictures, animated GIFs, and videos, short films, or movies. Audio files areal so getting increased attention on Tumblr and therefore might be a good area to potentially explore if your business lends itself to such. On Tumblr, a sound strategy to gain followers and attention is simply to follow others, preferably those within your target market. Tumblr does not display the number of people you are following, or, for that matter, the number of people who follow you. This enables you to safely get to know your audience and customize your own posts and content to suit their interests. It is even a platform that enables you to post, follow, or otherwise appreciate fan created content based on your products, services, or business - a flattering gesture demonstrating loyalty and spreading awareness for your company. In this way, you can engage customers by getting them directly involved and effectively enable them to do some of your advertising for you. If your contests for your followers to generate fan created content for you and offer a prize for the best creation, you will have an excellent promotion that is fun for everyone involved. I highly suggest letting the community vote on the best one in such competitions, making it an exciting experience even for those who do not directly participate. Any submissions can be used and appreciated in your own marketing campaigns, both on Tumblr and on other social media sites.

Like with Pinterest and Instagram, making things visually striking will really appeal to the Tumblr community. Unlike those two choices, however, hashtags are not an option on Tumblr, so you have to include compelling keywords to get your posts and content noticed. Aim to feature eye-catching pieces that trigger an emotional response, or something humorous, and you are likely to go far on Tumblr.

CHAPTER ELEVEN:
PAID SOCIAL MEDIA ADVERTISING

While promoting your business on Facebook, Twitter, Instagram or Pinterest can be accomplished with hard work and minimal expense, paid advertising on social media continue to grow exponentially. Facebook earns billions of dollars each year in ad revenue, with two-thirds of that income being generated from mobile advertising. Twitter earns hundreds of millions advertising revenue with 85% being generated by mobile advertising. So, while any business can promote their brand on their own inexpensively, it's safe to say that paid advertising on social media is highly effective and is driving the gigantic advertising revenue numbers from various social networking companies.

Paid social media ad expenses are justified by the fact that these ads garner 800-900% greater click-through frequency when compared to non-targeted website advertising. Likewise, paid promotional Tweets sustain much greater response when compared to regular website banner advertising.

For businesses and brands seeking real results, paid advertising on social media platforms is guaranteed to deliver. But using paid advertising doesn't have to replace the efforts you're making on your own; in fact, use what you learn from self-promoting on social media to refine your promotional messages for maximum effectiveness. By doing so, you'll get the most out of every paid advertising dollar that you spend.

Another benefit of paid social media advertising is the ability to highly target your audience. The reason that social media advertising is so successful is that messaging can be directed to a very specific target audience. Social media knows all about its users based on the information the users share in their profile; this information is used to target audiences and will always outperform general website advertising.

When purchasing social media advertising, do your research to gain an understanding of how each network prices its services. For example, Twitter bases its pricing on how the promoted tweets perform in driving the interaction between users and brands user interaction while Facebook and LinkedIn charge each time an ad is displayed (known as "per impression"). Advertisers should also consider that social media content is primarily consumed on smart phones. They should keep this factor in mind when designing advertisements.

CHAPTER TWELVE: FLICKR

Flickr is an online photo sharing service similar to Shutterfly, Snapfish and some of the other services that you use to upload and print your photos. Most people use these services to share their photo albums with their friends and family. However, marketers can use Flickr for more than just sharing photos.

Even though Flickr is not the largest photo sharing company, it is uniquely situated to benefit online internet marketers. Flickr has become the fastest growing online photo sharing service and is expected to continue to grow. Photo sharing allows you to upload and post photos online of your company, products, or services. Since Flickr is owned by Yahoo, it is featured prominently across the Yahoo network. For this reason, Flickr generates more search engine traffic than the other photo sharing sites, which makes it very beneficial for internet marketing.

Many online marketers are using Flickr to generate traffic and to get a high ranking with the search engines. Any picture that you upload can potentially have an audience of millions of users that could find your product and link back to your site. The key is content. The more relevant the content, to the content of your website or capture page, the more valuable a click on one of your photos will be. Take for example, displaying a photo of a house for sale. When someone clicks on your photo and then sees a capture page or web site with more houses for sale, they are more likely to visit your website than if the link was random.

What are the unique features that can help your photos drive traffic to your website? Each individual photo can get natural keyword rankings based on the content of the photo. The way to do this is by adding "tags" to your photo. For example, if you have a wholesale house for sale in Pompano Beach, you could add the following tags: house, house for sale, Pompano Beach, Pompano Beach house, foreclosure, short sale, house in Pompano Beach, etc.

You can add many tags for each photo. The more tags you add, the more that your photo will get natural rankings. Please keep in mind that for the natural rankings to be good, the keywords in the tag field need to be related. For example- foreclosure, real estate, short sale, are all related keywords, which are related to real estate.

Another key feature is that in addition to the tags, you have the opportunity to put information in the description. This is a perfect place for you to put a short bio, website, contact info, etc., to make it easier for people to find you if they are interested in your product or service.

You should use your company name or personal name, whichever you branded, as your user name and you can even change the icon (called buddy icon) to your logo or use your personal photo. By doing this, your username or company name is attached to each photo uploaded, which in itself, will generate natural rankings based on your name. Also, make sure that you take the time to edit your profile to include a description of yourself. Usually it is best to have a short bio along with a photo and a link back to your website and how to contact you. In other words, make sure your profile describes who you are, what you do, and how they can contact you.

Flickr allows you to create galleries so that you can divide your photos by groups into logical categories called sets. All of your photos can be displayed in your photo stream when someone clicks on your profile. Your photos are divided into collections, sets, and galleries. You can also add Flickr contacts and join groups related to your industry like other social networking sites.

While you are at that link, please note how I have used topic specific galleries and photos specific to one topic (real estate). Do not under any circumstance; mix your personal photos with your photo stream.

You can put personal photos on another service, like Shutterfly. Your Flickr account should be solely for the purpose of business marketing to promote your product, your services, or yourself. Flickr should be part of your social networking arsenal along with Facebook, Twitter, LinkedIn, and YouTube.

You could also use this service as a picture host for pictures on your websites and capture pages. If adding a lot of pictures, you will eventually have to upgrade your account to a pro account.

If you have a blog or blogs, you can automatically post a link on your blog to your Flickr photos directly from your Flickr account. Simply click on any photo in your photo stream and click on "blog this" at the top and your photo will appear on your blog (or blogs if you have more than one).

You can also setup applications like Twitter directly from Flickr using third party applications. You can post a link to your Flickr photos on Twitter directly from Flickr using the "Flickr 2 Twitter" application. This process works exactly the same as posting to the blogs. You can visit the "app garden" in Flickr for a list of third party applications. Another useful application from Flickr is Flickr tab for Facebook which you add directly from your Flickr account or by their website link from Facebook at: *http://www.facebook.com/flickrtab*.

CHAPTER THIRTEEN:
BLOGS

B logs used to be called web logs. Eventually users dropped the "w" and "e" and web logs became known as blogs. A blog is a regularly maintained diary or journal that is posted on the internet for everyone to see. People that post entries in these online journals are called bloggers. Writing entries and posting them online is called blogging. Blogging is extremely prolific and there are over 200 million blogs worldwide. It seems that many people that are online have something to say. Most blogs do not serve any commercial business purpose and are simply ramblings or online diaries (many are teenagers). However, some bloggers have turned blogging into big business.

The following is a list of the top ten blogs based on traffic for today. Because blogs are not static but are dynamically changing every day the rankings change every day. However, each one of these blogs gets tremendous traffic, which is what I am trying to illustrate. Don't make the mistake of thinking that a blog is only for teenager's that want an online diary. While some blogs are exactly that, the ones below will show you the commercial and business implication of a professional blog. Imagine if you had a blog like one of these below for your business. This list is compiled by: *www.technorati.com*.

. Top Ten Blogs

1. *http://www.huffingtonpost.com*
2. *http://www.buzzfeed.com*
3. *http://www.gawker.com*
4. *http://mashable.com*

5. *http://businessinsider.com*

6. *http://www.tmz.com*

7. *http://www.arstechnica.com*

8. *http://www.techcrunch.com*

9. *http://www.theverge.com*

10. *http://www.gizmodo.com*

Most of the above blogs are political or technological. However, notice how professional they are. These are professional blogs that generate huge traffic and revenue. One that is interesting to follow if you are an internet marketer is number 4, which is *http://mashable. com*. If you want to be up to date with the latest online internet marketing techniques, follow this blog.

Blogging is what we had before there was Twitter. The difference is that with Twitter your message is limited to 140 characters. With blogging you can ramble on as much as you need or want to. If other people find what you say to be of relevance, they will follow your blog. As they do so your blog will rise in popularity and be read by many more people. Your blog will then begin to be featured and linked to by other bloggers writing about similar topics. However, it will take effort on your part to continuously add content to your blog and to make it interesting enough for users to want to return.

Opening a blog is free. There are three main blogging companies. They are *www.blogger.com,www.wordpress.com,* and *www.typepad. com*. Lately Typepad has not been as popular and WordPress seems to be the blog host of choice. Blogger is a little easier to use than Word Press, but I recommend that you use Word Press for a more professional look. Also, WordPress is gaining much more traffic than Blogger. I suggest you open up a blog first on blogger to see how blogging works. Then when you understand the concept, open up a Word PressBlog. In the website section, I recommended that your entire website be a WordPress Blog. By doing this, you will have a professional looking site and you will be able to add content slowly.

Make sure your blog theme matches that of your website or as mentioned above, have your website and blog be the same site.

Your blog should have many links from your blog back to your website, social networking links, articles that you have written etc. All of these should link from your blog back to your website. It is important to have your blogs RSS feed incorporate into your website so that your website content is fresh and changing.

- You should have the following links on your blog
- Twitter icon with a link to your Twitter profile
- LinkedIn icon with a link to your LinkedIn Profile
- Facebook icon with a link to your Facebook profile
- YouTube icon with a link to your YouTube profile
- RSS Icon with a link to your RSS feeds
- Flickr Icon with a link to your Flickr Profile

Also, make sure that you get your blog listed in all of the blog directories like blog catalog, bloghub etc. (There are hundreds of directories). There are companies like, *http://www.submitinme. com* that will submit your blog to multiple blog directories for a small fee. Make a good description about your blog and give it to a company, like the one mentioned above, and you will have many blog links back to your website. Since they are based in India and English is not their first language, type out exactly what you want in your blog description before submitting your blog details to them. Also, establish a specific Google Gmail address for them to use for this purpose.

If you want to appear more professional with your blog and are computer savvy, I recommend looking into hosting your own WordPress blog, on your own domain. Decent computer skills are required to do this, but it is not that difficult and well worth the effort. You can control the look and feel of your blog much more when you are creating the entire design of it. Or have your web designer design your web site in WordPress and have someone show you how to post blog entries on your site by yourself.

You have control of which applications to use. You can download a version of Word press from *http://wordpress.org/*. Please note that

157

this is not the same as *http://wordpress.com* which is a free shared hosting blog. Wordpress.org is not as easy to use as Wordpress. com. You will need to learn how to use "plug- ins", which are third party applications. However, these "plug-ins will allow you to have much more control of your blog than a shared hosting blog like on Wordpress.com. This is especially important if you want to start incorporating search engine optimization, social networking integration.

The main difference of why to bother with Wordpress.org is the way Google indexes their search engines. You see blogs by definition have constantly changing content because the owner of the blog is "blogging" which means constantly writing things and posting them online. Because blogs have much more content change than websites, Google indexes them higher on the search rankings. For this reason, a blog will register better on the search engines than a website will.

I have heard more than one internet marketer refer to the word "blog" standing for "better listings on Google". Having a WordPress. org blog allows you to create a blog that looks like a website. Users will not know that your site is a blog, but Google will. Your site will rank higher and get more traffic. That reason combined with the abundance of free applications and "plug-ins" is why Wordpress.Org is so popular with professional bloggers.

Captivate with the Written Word

Although maintaining a blog doesn't constitute social networking in the most modern sense, blogging as a practice can so often act as the cornerstone of a great social media marketing strategy. As a central and stable hub for sharing detailed and valuable information with your audience and having them share it with others. A blog is not only a fantastic way to build authority within your business niche, but also a place to re-purpose social media content, amplify your brand's voice, personality, and core values, and ultimately sell to a legion of engaged customers. When people share your content, Google listens. The more your blog posts are shared, the better your site will rank in search engines and the more traffic will find its way to you. Of course, there are a ton more factors that go into making a blog successful, such as website SEO, plugins, copywriting skills, and more, way more than I can cover here. Instead, this chapter will explore some of the ways that you can prepare your blog for the social world and reveal some of the best types of content to create in order to captivate your audience.

Integrate social sharing into your blog; include a call to action

No blog worth its salt will forgo the installation of good, clear social sharing widgets to allow users to easily share its content to the biggest social networks including Facebook, Twitter, and Pinterest. Even the best bloggers in the world don't have their work found without a little help from their readers. You need to empower people to easily share your blog posts with their social connections. Visit any popular blog and you'll see an array of social sharing options above or below (or above and below) each post, often coupled with a call to action to encourage people to hit "Like", "Tweet" or "Share." There are plenty of ways to install and customize the way your blog's social sharing buttons display, some of which we've already covered earlier in the book, but one of the easiest and most popular options is through Add This (*http://www.addthis.com*). This is a plugin that will place the buttons on your page in just a few clicks. In addition to the established social media sharing options, provide a 'Subscribe via RSS' button in a prominent place on your page, so that people can have your posts pushed to them in their Google Reader or RSS feed as soon as they are published.

Ways to encourage social sharing and encourage engagement also extend to the blog content itself, whether it's through pre-populated tweets containing valuable snippets of the article's information.

Click to Tweet (*http://clicktotweet.com/*will facilitate that) or teasing the article but not revealing all of it until they share your link (the WordPress plugin SocialLocker does this). As the latter requires people to act before they have even read your content, I would use it with great caution, reserved for premium content you believe people will desperately want to see.

Produce top content, make some of it evergreen

First and foremost, always aim to produce inspiring and educational content on a regular basis that is shareable. At the core of many great blogs is a set of evergreen posts (articles that will never go out of date or are updated periodically to make sure that they won't). Evergreen blog posts can act as the backbone of your brand and its expertise online, position you as an authority figure with your finger on the pulse, and help to drive interest in your company. The types of evergreen posts that do best include articles that are written to help beginners (the people most likely to be searching online for assistance), e.g., "The Complete Beginner's Guide to Choosing Your First Electric Car," and ones that answer FAQs, e.g., "Is Paragliding Safe? Here's Everything You Need to Know." As I mentioned above, be sure to revisit these posts from time to time to keep them up to date and the definitive online resource for whatever the topic might be. To promote evergreen content and gives its visitors a clear point of reference, think about creating something like a "Start Here" page, a menu link to training guides, or a "Top posts" widget in the sidebar of your site.

Write effective headlines: be clear and concise

Learn to write keyword – rich headlines that will make people want to read the rest of your article, especially if all they have to go on is the blog post title, they see in a list of search results or within a tweet. Don't try to be too clever or cryptic with your headlines; be as clear and direct about what the post will offer someone who might come across it e.g.,"Hot or Cold? The Experts Tell All" is pretty ambiguous next to something like "Hot or Cold Water? Expert Opinion on How to Shower." Some tried and tested ideas for powerful headlines include asking questions, e.g., "How Do I Craft Amazing Blog Post Headlines?", teasing content to attract click-through, e.g., "When one man's son was on the brink of flunking college, three words changed his whole life around...", or making references that tie your content into readers' interests or scenarios they often encounter.

"This is how America's #1 Mom Potty Trained Her Kids in 24 Hours." Think about which keywords your customers will be using to find the content that you provide and replicate them in your blog post titles. A customer is much more likely to search for "how to bake chocolate cake recipe" rather than "Om nom nom, check out our great chocolate cake recipe". Your heading might read, "Recipe: How to Bake A Delicious Chocolate Cake."

Popular blog post frameworks for highly-readable posts

Sometimes you'll have the best idea for the subject of a blog post, but trouble finding a way to structure it in a way that is concise, clear, and easily read by you audience. Here is a variety of common ways to give a framework to your blog post ideas:

Versus posts

The power of the Internet has given consumers more choice than ever when it comes to buying products and services, or deciding between one idea or another, so much so that the decision is often overwhelming. A great way to solve this dilemma, and put together a great blog post, is the X vs. Y article. For example, a company that specializes in beds and mattresses might write a blog post explaining the pros and cons of sprung mattresses as opposed to memory foam. Similarly, "What is the best X?" types of posts work in a like fashion. These types of posts help consumers make a sound decision, make you stand out as a trustworthy authority figure, and are easy to put together.

Problem-solving posts

One of the main reasons that people search online is to find solutions to their problems, whether seeking to learn how to sew a button back on to their shirt, how to house train their dog, or how a guy makes himself irresistible to the opposite sex. Focusing on the solution to problems, especially for businesses, is a great way to come up with new ideas for blog posts and attract web traffic. Think about the problems that your customers want to solve and then use your expertise to tell them how you or your business can help. To use dogs as an example, a pet store owner might blog about the best way to stop your dog from barking, or how to teach it to sit or fetch. Think about how you can become an invaluable resource for your customers and for those searching for solutions to their problems on the Internet.

List posts

'List posts' are extremely popular in almost any industry, as they can be read quickly and are great for sharing, e.g., 10 Top Marketing Tips For Your Blog. There are three common types of list post: Brief list posts are long, bulleted snippets of information that users can use as a platform to search for more detailed information elsewhere (sometimes useful, but not always the best way to keep readers engaged on your site!), detailed list posts provide more complex, valuable information-like these tips, and hybrid posts lie somewhere in the middle.

Break news, offer opinion, and ask questions

Writing blog posts about breaking news within your industry sector is not only one of the best ways to come up with new and original content, but it also positions you as an authority figure in the eyes of readers. However, rather than simply regurgitating a press release or something you found on a big news site, frame your story in a way that makes it relevant to your audience, positions you as an authority, and encourages people to interact: offer an opinion, and ask readers to share their own as a way to drive engagement. One of the easiest ways to illicit a response is to close your blog posts with a simple request, e.g., "What do you guys think? Tell us in the comments". You'll be surprised how much interaction this garners up, especially if the question you ask is simple and quick to answer.

Spin hot or detailed topics into multiple posts

One of the biggest challenges many bloggers face, is creating fresh content, week in, week out. One of the techniques you can use to combat this is called "spinning". In a nutshell, it involves taking one important topic that you know your audience will lap up and writing about it from a variety of different standpoints. Let's take an article about painting a garden fence, for example. Several different blog posts about that one topic might be: 'A Beginner's Guide to Painting a Garden Fence'; '5 of the Biggest Garden Fence Painting Mistakes';

'Video: How to Paint a Garden Fence in 5 Easy Steps', or 'How [Brand X] is Revolutionizing Garden Fence Painting'. Get the idea? Drilling down on individual topics like this, as opposed to being more general, maybe beneficial in terms of attracting people hunting for more specific information or advice.

Guest posting

Offer to write guest posts on other influential bloggers' blogs and provide a link back to your own blog at the bottom of the post in return, as part of the agreement. This is particularly useful if you manage to post on a blog that is much more popular than yours! As well as guest posting on other blogs yourself, be open-minded about other experts posting on yours to help build a strong network of friends within your industry.

Celebrate milestones

As traffic to your blog grows, celebrate this in specific blog posts, thanking readers for their continued support. Use these posts to highlight your most popular content so far, to encourage new readers to go back and revisit, increasing page views and time on your site.

Note: In an online world packed with strong opinions, research-backed blog posts are often more persuasive, and therefore popular, than those that are solely story based. Quoting authoritative resources, citing statistics and studies, or even showcasing your own data, can be an effective way to back up your arguments, emanate credibility, and create stellar blog content that stands out from the competition. For example, which blog post title would you be most likely to click on from the following: "How to Run Faster and More Efficiently" or "How to Run 20% Faster and More Efficiently in 4 Weeks"? Where the circumstances call for it, the data-backed title will always win out.

Use awesome images in your blog posts

As I discussed in the Facebook Tips chapter of this book, social networks like Facebook (and Google+) will pull in a photo from your blog to display when someone shares your blog link. If the photo is poor or there isn't one at all, then there is little chance of your plain link catching the eyes of people browsing through their news feeds. One blog post image is good, but several are even better. Multiple images within a blog post help to break up long blocks of text, make your articles more memorable, and can be used to enhance a written fact or opinion. Check out the "Explained: The Best Types of Content to Post on Social Media" chapter for advice on where to find, and how to use great images.

Note: Adding alternative text (alt-text) to images is not just important for search engine optimization (they can't see pictures but do grab the text and include it in image searches), but it also acts as the description of images pinned to Pinterest. Alt-text is what pops up when you hover your cursor over an image and it can be edited in the image upload process on most blogging platforms, including WordPress and Blogger.

Encourage email subscriptions

The harsh truth is that when someone has visited your blog once, there is a good chance that they will not return for a second visit. To combat this, you need to position yourself to target these people in future at a location where it is hard to ignore you, their email inbox. By gathering email addresses, you have a ready pool of willing contacts with whom you can share new blog posts and updates and slowly help to convert them into more passionate brand ambassadors. In addition to placing a box for people to sign up to your newsletter, in a prominent position on your home page, also add a sign-up box to the bottom of a handful of your most popular blog posts from the past (use Analytics to find out which these are). Be sure to let visitors know what they are signing up for before they hit 'Submit' so that your emails are not considered spam and consider including a discount code or free gift (like a PDF guide) as a way to sweeten the deal.

Add names, titles and bio to build authority and trust

It is common for readers to want to contact and communicate with the author of a great blog post after they have finished reading it, and not just in the comments section. Bios and bylines also add authority and trust to the blog post with which they are associated, so be sure to include your name, title, and contact information at the bottom of each of your blog posts. Customers can then follow or contact you.

The blog post length

There is always plenty of debate about the optimum length of a blog post, particularly when you are dealing with an audience who is short of time, who can easily look elsewhere, and are forever skimming quickly through content. I would suggest forgetting about the word count, at least to a degree. Instead, focus on creating interesting, well-formatted content that web and mobile readers will love, whether it takes 100 words or 1,000 (do note, however, that long form content generally has less competition). The overall quality of the post should not be dictated by its length.

Use descriptive URLs for SEO

For improved SEO, ensure every blog post URL is descriptive rather than just functional, e.g., *www.yoursite.com/10-top-blogging-tips-for-business.htm,* instead of *www.yoursite.com/post345.htm.* On most blogging platforms, the URL is normally generated from the words used in the blog post's title. If you're able to edit the URL to make it even more optimized for SEO and think it can be improved over what has been automatically generated, go ahead and do it.

The 'deep linking' and 'linking to other sites' trick

Whenever you refer to a previous blog post while writing, be sure to add a hyperlink to it, so that readers can go back and check it out. On that note, you want readers to stay on your page as long as possible, so if you link outside of your website for any reason, be sure to set the link to open in a new window.

Make your blog mobile-friendly

As an ever-increasing number of people browse the web using smartphones and tablets, they are hugely significant in the way

165

you design your blog's visual layout and write its content. Some of the biggest free blog providers (including Blogger and WordPress) will automatically display their blogs into a mobile-friendly format, so make sure yours does too. From a mobile user's view, there is nothing more off-putting than clicking onto a blog, only to have to keep zooming and scrolling to read the text. Try to avoid writing in long and complex sentences and avoid extremely long paragraphs at all costs. Web readers have a limited attention span and skim articles, but mobile users are likely to be even more distracted. If you are writing a long post, be sure to break it up into short paragraphs with individual headings in order to make it as digestible as possible.

Share and re-purpose your blog post for maximum exposure

1. Get shares from industry influencers

Not all shares are created equal. If you want to encourage your awesome blog content to be a runaway hit, think about how much easier this would be if you could get influential people within your field to share your link with their hundreds or thousands of loyal fans. The best way to go about this is to work backwards. Spend time building a relationship with the influencer(s) first, by commenting on their own blog, tweeting them to ask a question about their work or for a quote to use in your work, etc. At the same time, also analyze the type of content they are already sharing, so that you can reflect this in your own posts. This strategy works because people love to share things they've been involved in, even if they weren't directly responsible for putting it together.

2. Re-share evergreen content

As mentioned near the beginning of this book, automation on social media can, in the right circumstances, be very beneficial to you, a time saver, and a chance to give the content you slaved over as much exposure as possible. One case where this is certainly true is the automated scheduling and posting of evergreen blog content across multiple social networks, which can help to extend its useful life over and over again. For example, you could tweet a link to the same blog article two or three times in the same week, then keep the same frequency for the next few months using alternative post titles to see which performs best. Some ways that you might want to restyle a social media post featuring the same blog article, as an alternative to [post title] + [link], include: posing a question as a lead into the post, quoting a striking sentence or statistic from the article, or showing off just a little, e.g., "Our most popular read from last month..." My tool of choice is Buffer (*http://www.bufferapp.com*), which allows you to bulk-upload and organize content to be posted to Facebook, Twitter, Google+ and LinkedIn at a date and time of your choosing.

Monitor progress with Google Analytics

Use Google Analytics to monitor the volume and quality of search terms, which drive visitors to your site. Use the information you find to tailor the direction of new content, expand on the most popular topics and tweak or ditch those that aren't working quite as well. Check your Analytics regularly to ensure you're always in tune with what your readers like and want.

CHAPTER FOURTEEN:
REDDIT

Known as the internet's frontpage, Reddit has been growing in popularity exponentially since the past few years. It's a news outlet site where the users either up vote or down vote content to the top of the front page. The site's userbase, for the most part, is active and engaged with whatever's going on around the world. Many people's personal sites that make it to the front page of Reddit crash because of the insane amounts of traffic overloading their servers. With that kind of traffic, you can easily get website viewers and potential customers.

Unfortunately, getting to the first page of Reddit itself takes hard work and a ton of luck, but luckily, you don't have to get to the front page of Reddit to route their traffic to your website. In fact, Reddit has these things called sub-reddits which are "smaller" Reddit sites within the main website.

In recent years, Reddit has grown exponentially as a digital marketing tool with its effectiveness in market research, lead generation, and promotion being a key reason for its recent importance in digital marketing circles.

You can easily build a solid foundation for brand exposure and promotion by contributing to communities that discuss products and services related to your niche. By simply offering input or showing your expertise on a topic, your brand is guaranteed to attract engagement.

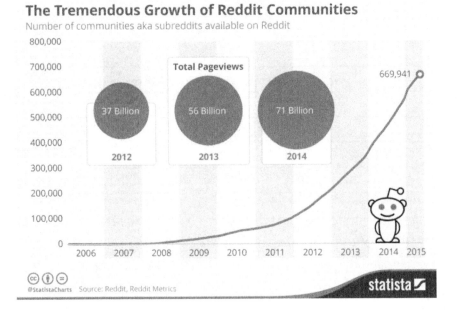

The Tremendous Growth of Reddit Communities
Number of communities aka subreddits available on Reddit

The influence of Reddit communities on a brand's presence cannot be underestimated. Between engagement numbers and page views, it is clear to see that the platform can be crucial in expanding your business reach.

Subreddits, for example, are very theme specific and easier to rank high in. Within this report, I'll show you how to harness the traffic of sub-reddits to drive insane amounts of traffic to your website. It'll take a bit of dedication, time, and a hint of luck. There's no reason that you can't at least rank on the first page of a sub-reddit for your niche. It's not hard at all, but many people are misinformed about how to use Reddit for marketing, which Reddit is against. What I'm about to teach you how get your highly engaged viewers while completely abiding by Reddit's T.O.S.

Requirements to Market on Reddit

Although I said that marketing on Reddit is easy, you need a few skills to market effectively on your own. You could get around some of the things that I'm about to say you need, but it'll cost money to outsource or learn. Anyways, I'll get into the things you'll need to market or promote your website on Reddit.

The things you'll need are:

- English Language Composition, Comprehension, and Reading Skills at a Proficient Level
- A Couple of Minutes a Day
- Article Writing Skills (for your website)

The reason you'll need all of the English components above is because the main language spoken on Reddit is English. If you can't write in at least a high school English level, then your ability to communicate will make you seem more like a "marketer." Even though you are trying to market on Reddit, you don't want to appear as one because people hate marketers on Reddit.

To get back on topic, you'll need to know how to communicate with people on Reddit in English at an at least high school level, for at least 3days. I'll get into this later, but it is a necessity. The next thing you'll need is a couple of minutes of spare time a day to interact with other threads on Reddit. Again, this is where your English skills come into play. It won't take long, but you'll still need a few minutes to start building a small 'identity' for your Reddit account. I'll go into this in detail later.

The last things you'll need are article writing skills. I'm assuming that you want to drive traffic to your website, and the easiest way to do this with Reddit is with article marketing. You could substitute this with a video if you think you're better off with making a video.

You could always outsource the article or video for $5 on *http:// www.Fiverr.com*, but I have a secret up my sleeve that'll make writing an article easy. You don't even have to come up with the idea or topic of the article. I'll go into it later, but you can decide whether you want to write your own article or video or outsource. With that being said, if you have all of the necessary skills, you should be able to move on to the actual method.

Marketing with Reddit Made Easy

So, without rambling for over 20 pages, I'll get straight into the method itself. The first thing you'll need, of course, is a Reddit account. You can easily create one at *http://www.reddit.com*. Make sure the username you choose doesn't sound 'spammy.' You'll want it to sound generic. On all the other social media sites, having a username related to your niche is completely fine and what you're supposed to do. However, on Reddit, you'll want to appear to be 'an average Joe.' I can't stress the fact that people hate marketers, yet they download their content, nearly instantly on Reddit enough.

Something simple like your first name + your favorite animal + some number will be fine.

Once you have your Reddit account, you'll want to appear to be engaged with the niche you're trying to tap traffic from. For instance, if you had a news site about gaming then you would want to type the word gaming into the search bar on the front of Reddit. Look for some sub-reddits that are similar to what you're into. In the example's case, /r/gaming seems to be a good one for now. You could always find more sub-reddits, but to keep this report short and to the point, I'll only be using one sub-reddit.

Now that you've collected your list of sub-reddit(s), you'll want to explore each one and find posts that hopefully interest you. On those posts, you'll want to drop a meaningful comment. You will also want to comment on comments by other people. Make yourself seem like an engaged user of the community. It'll make you look less like a marketer, and more like a user. I highly suggest doing this for at least three days because it prevents you from getting ghosted.

Being 'ghosted' means that only you (on your IP address) will see the content you post or submit. That means that whatever you submit is useless because nobody else gets to use it. If Reddit's algorithms suspect that you're only making a Reddit account to promote your content, then they'll automatically ghost you. The worst part is that you won't know you're getting ghosted unless you have a VPN or IP changing to check on the links you post. Anyways, you can completely avoid the ghosting situation altogether if you just interact with the communities and sub-reddits you're trying to post in. At least three days of commenting and interacting should be good enough. Commenting and interacting shouldn't take more than five minutes a day, but it can easily be done in two minutes.

While you have a bunch of down time, because you only have to comment occasionally, you should start getting a viral article written. This is a lot easier than people thing. Just head on over to *https:// news.google.com/* and type in your niche name. Once you do that, just search through all of the articles until you find something that genuinely sounds interesting or 'click bait 'worthy.

Click the article and give it a read through. If it sounds like great and viral content, you're good to go. Just rewrite or rephrase every single sentence and upload it to your blog. It's that easy. Assuming that you type at an average 30 to 40 words per minute, you should be able to rewrite and type up the article in less than 30minutes.

You may be thinking that this is copying, and for the most part, its kind of is. However, think about any viral story on the news or internet. That story appears on every single popular news show, radio show, and website. The only difference is that it's rephrased. To sum it up, you're not doing anything wrong by rephrasing and paraphrasing the ENTIRE article. You're essentially speaking from your own words. If you really are worried about plagiarism, then you could cite your source at the bottom of the article, but it would be overkill. The bottom line is that you're fine with rewriting it in your own words.

So, now that you have an article, simple upload it to the site you're trying to drive traffic to. It would be wise at this point to add in your ads and affiliate offers. Once that's finished, you're about 90% done. Make sure that the article you publish on your website has an attractive header or title. It wouldn't be a bad thing if it was a little bit 'click baity'. The point is to grab people's attentions.

Now, hopefully at least three days of commenting on your Reddit account went by. You're now read to submit a link. Go to the subreddit you want to drive traffic to your website and submit a link submission. You'll want it to be a link submission because you want people to click the link and go to your site directly. The other submission will allow you to paste your article. That will allow people to read your article without having to go to your site. You lose potential customers and ad revenue if you do that route; instead stick with link posts.

After finishing that, give yourself a round of applause. You did it! Your article is now in the subreddit and niche you wanted. All you have to do now is wait for traffic to come to your website. Even if you don't hit the first page of your subreddit, you should still see quite a number of people visit your website through the link on Reddit. The more high-quality and engaging the article is, the more likely it is to be upvoted and shared on Reddit. If you don't make the front page of your subreddit the first time, don't be discouraged. Just keep writing articles and repeating the method. In fact, you don't even need to create a new Reddit account, since the account you made is completely 'natural'. Just keep making regular posts to build your authority and you can continue to post article links to your website.

Not only are you going to get traffic to your website, but you'll also reap the great SEO value from Reddit for each article that you submit. It's a win-win either way. As long as you're consistent with your commenting and posting, then you should be getting traffic and SEO value directed back to your site.

CHAPTER FIFTEEN:
RSS FEEDS

If you look on most blogs will see a little orange square. That is the symbol for RSS Feeds, which you should take the time to learn and understand. RSS stands for "really simple syndication", which is another way of saying "spread your message across the internet". Having your message in an RSS feed which can be picked up by feed readers is called syndication. They can be read using an RSS reader or feed reader. RSS Feeds also appear in your "favorites" tab on your internet explorer toolbar, which allows you to save favorite RSS feeds, like you would save favorite websites. RSS feeds have unique URL's (web addresses) like websites do.

Feeds have an RSS or XML at the end of the URL and feeds always look the same, so they are easy to identify. The feeds strip away all the graphics from the website and keep only the text-based items, which can then be read by a reader, built into your web browser. Your Twitter profile has an RSS feed. As well as your Facebook, your blog, your LinkedIn, You Tube, Ezine Article, Podcast, etc.

Almost every website that has updated content has an RSS feed. Standard websites do not have updated content since they are static, and the content never changes. Blogs, Ezine articles, news sites, Facebook or anywhere where the content changes will not be static and will have an RSS feed. Almost every social networking site and blog has an RSS Feeder and these RSS feeds should link into your website. This gives you two benefits. First, it allows people to find your website via the reader. Second, it gives dynamic changing content to your website which makes your website rank higher than other static websites in the search engine rankings.

Don't forget to submit your RSS feeds to as many sites as possible that allow submit RSS feeds like,*www.Feedster.com,* or *www. friendfeed.com,*or the hundreds of other feed sites out there. If you would rather have someone submit the RSSfeeds to directories for you, then use a company like,*www.submitinme.com* or one of the many other websites that will submit RSS feeds for a fee.

CHAPTER SIXTEEN: POSTLETS.COM

This chapter is specifically for real estate investors and realtors, wholesalers or anyone that would like to sell a house or offer real estate for sale. This website is a classic example of how to integrate websites and social networking to drive traffic to your listing and ultimately generate more revenue.*www.postlets.com,* is a fantastic way to offer your real estate for sale to a very diverse audience for free. Postlets is now owned by Zillow which is a huge plus since Zillow is the most trafficked real estate website on the planet. I encourage you to visit the ,*www.postlets.com,*website if you are a realtor, wholesaler, or real estate investor that would like to sell a house or houses.

When you submit a house for sale on *postlets.com,* you receive a free listing page that lists all pertinent information about the house including the address, photos, description, local schools, maps, etc. The postlets page is basically a one-page flyer of your property. It looks similar to an MLS listing sheet. You can print out this one page and put it on display at real estate events. The website allows you to copy the html from your online flyer and paste it into any other website that allows html coding. This means you can instantly put your flyer on Craigslist, Backpage, and any other online site that accepts html.

The unique thing about postlets is that they syndicate your listing to multiple websites for free. For example, your listing is automatically syndicated to many other websites that are specifically related to real estate including Zillow, Trulia, Hot Pads, By Owner MLS and many others. And the best part is that postlets is completely free.

Another added benefit of why I really like *www.postlets.com,*is that you are offered the ability to market your listing via social networking. This feature is what makes this website so amazing for real estate investors, realtors and wholesalers. You can log into your postlets account and share your postlets information by giving *postlets.com* access to your social networking sites like Facebook and Twitter. For example, you could post on Twitter: "wholesale deal 3 bed 2 bath in Hollywood" and then you can put a link to your postlets page where you have an online flyer on the property. This is a very effective technique to generate buyers, especially if there is a capture page when they click on your link.

Postlets offers a really incredible way to drive traffic to your listings for free. If you are a real estate agent that has many houses to sell, then simply creating a postlets account and then syndicating your postlet listing to all your various social networking sites is a great way to get maximum visibility for your listings. The same applies if you are a landlord looking for tenants. If you are in the business of selling real estate, I will go so far as to say that you cannot afford not to have a postlets account. I say this because this is one of the best freeways to syndicate your listings to multiple social networking sites.

As mentioned before, you can even create a Craigslist posting directly from your postlets account. You can then utilize the html feature to post to multiple classified ad websites that allow html coding like for example,*www.Craigslist.com,www.Oodle.com,www.Backpage.com, www.Ebay.com, www.Kijiji.com,www.Olx.com.*

Think of it as free marketing that drives traffic back to your site. Of course, when this traffic gets to your site you will have a capture page that captures their information. This is a great way to build a buyers list. For example, my capture page says that we have many bank owned properties for sale. Every one of my postlets listings has my capture page listed twice in each listing. Then this postlet page gets syndicated to multiple social networking sites as well as to sites like Craigslist, Backpage, eBay, Kijiji, Oodle, Olx, etc. I can literally create hundreds of links on the internet for just one house listing.

This creates a lot of traffic to my website which in turn converts into buyers which are captured in my database. The best feature of *postlets.com,* is that you're able to have up to eighteen pictures of a on a mini website of your own.

CHAPTER SEVENTEEN: ONLINE CLASSIFIED ADS

M any people have already heard about the Craigslist phenomena. In case you didn't know, Craigslist is the most trafficked free online classified ad website on the planet, according to January 2017 statistics. Craigslist is currently the 11 most visited website in the United States beating WordPress and Linked-In. You need to take notice of Craigslist and the amazing amount of traffic that it generates. You might have already known about Craigslist, but did you know that there are literally thousands of online classified ad websites? There are thousands of websites all over the world with classified ads in almost every language.

For our purposes of internet marketing, we are primarily interested in the English language websites with high U.S traffic. In order to filter through all of the websites, I have included only those classified ad sites with an Alexa ranking (*http://www.alexa.com*) of 50,000 or less. In addition to this, the list below is only for those websites with U.S Traffic. Most of the websites on this list have extremely high traffic with a very high Alexa ranking. For example, many people are not familiar with *www.backpage.com,* but according to *www. alexa.com*, Backpage is the 173rd most visited website in the Unites States. *www.Kijiji.com* is another website owned by eBay (now called eBay Classifieds) that many people are not familiar with which ranks currently as the 1043rd most visited website in the U.S. Below is the list of the most trafficked US classified ad websites.

Classified Ad Websites with High U.S Traffic as of January 2017.

1. Craigslist
2. OLX

3. Kijiji

4. VendAnything.com

5. Clickooz

6. FreeTicketClassifieds.com

7. American listed

8. Locate FreeClassifieds

9. Backpage.com

10. WorldStuffer

11. TocalAds.com

12. Gumtree.com

13. VooClick.com

14. Vivastreet.org

15. ViewMyClassified.com

Many of the above websites will allow you to copy and paste html. If you are in the business of real estate and selling houses, then you can really drive a lot of traffic to your website by using *www.postlets. com,* which we spoke about in the previous chapter. As mentioned in that chapter, if you post a listing on *postlets.com* then your listing creates a flyer in html which can be posted on classified ad websites like Craigslist, Backpage, Kijiji, etc.

By copying the html created from your *postlet.com* flyer, you could post to every free classified ad website that allows html. Since there are so many sites, you can create literally hundreds of postings. For example, imagine you are a Realtor® that has ten listings for sale. If creating a postlet account, copy the html for the flyer of your listing and post it to Craigslist. Then you can also post the same flyer to Backpage, Kijiji, etc.

Assume you posted that one listing to twenty classified ad websites. You would now have twenty references to that property on the web. Now, if you repeated that same process for the other nine listings, you would have a total often properties multiplied by twenty listings for a total of two hundred references to your properties. Each one of these references will have a link back to your website along with a description of your business and how to contact you. If you now incorporate this with a capture page, it can be extremely powerful.

You will be surprised at how many people contact you when you place an ad like this. You can repeat the same process of a dummy ad but make it better by building a professional dummy ad with an actual house for sale that is really cheap. Use this house to create a flyer in, *postlets.com*, and then copy and paste this html into multiple free classified ad websites.

Make sure that a link to your capture page is predominantly displayed and easy to follow. Your link should be something like: "Click here for more deals like this". When they click on the link, they should be taken to a capture page where you can add them to your database. Please see the chapter on capture pages and the chapter on databases to understand how this process works.

Please remember that although this chapter is about online classified ads, you should employ the exact same tactics in regular classified ads in the newspaper to build your buyers list. Many older people that have lots of cash are not online. Don't forget that there are still a lot of people that do not have computers and are not online.

Also, in addition to free classified ad websites there are many websites that are not free but where it is worthwhile to post wholesale deals and to find more buyers. One example is Ebay.com. It will cost $150 to list a property but you will generate a tremendous amount of traffic. Please remember that if you are posting an ad for something that does not appear to be a great bargain you will not generate much traffic.

You should wait until you have a wholesale house or listing at a very cheap price where you know that listing will get a lot of attention. This will usually be a wholesale deal for a house at a wholesale price and not a retail price. It also works best for a cheap house. For example, a house in Fort Lauderdale for $30,000 is going to get a lot of attention because many people know where Fort Lauderdale is, and they are curious about the house and why it is so cheap.

Remember that your ad should be for a cheap house at a wholesale price (65% of what the house is really worth). The house has to appear to be a great bargain if you want people to notice it. If you list your phone number and people call, then make sure to save all the phone numbers of everyone who calls and return their calls before adding them to your buyers list.

CHAPTER EIGHTEEN: MEETUP.COM

Meetup.com is a phenomenal success story that has enjoyed rapid success and for good reason. *www.meetup.com,* allows anyone to set up a meeting for a group of people with shared common interests. These meetings are called "meetups" hence the name Meetup.com. There are meetup groups for almost any sport, hobby, or activity that you can think of. Attending meet ups is a great way to meet people with common interests but as far as networking for business is concerned, meetups can be a phenomenal way to drive new business.

The important thing with Meetup.com and how it is different from other social networking sites is that you have to have face to face interaction at least once a month. That is one of the key differences with this form of marketing than with all of the other social and online marketing methods in this book. In order to host a meeting at least once a month, you will need to have something to share with your audience that can benefit them. Note how I said them and not you.

Running a meetup.com group will not in itself generate revenue, but it will drive more business and you will be considered an industry expert and go to person in your field of expertise. Try and think of it as giving first and receiving later. If you set up your meetup and then try and sell your audience without giving them information, I can promise that you will fail. No one will be at your next meeting. However, if you give tons of free information and make it informative and a good place to network and make friends then people will keep coming back. The reason that my club grew so rapidly was that for the first two years all we did was give free information. People came to our club and received a lot of free education about investing in real estate. That is what made them keep coming back.

It is okay for you to sell something and there is nothing wrong with having a product or service to sell. However, just remember that they are there to learn, to network and to be educated. If they want to buy your product or service, then they will. If not, then let them network.

Here are some examples of how you could use meetup.com to generate more business.

A real estate staging company could hold monthly Meetups on how to stage your home for a quick sale. This could be interspersed with ideas for decorating your house, furnishings, etc. When the participants want to stage their home, they are more likely to ask the staging company whose meetup they attend regularly. Why? The reason is because they have established a relationship. Lasting relationships are very important to new business. If your business is thriving, then you only need to maintain your relationships. But if trying to generate new business, then focus on creating relationships. Meetup.com is a very effective way to do this.

A Title Insurance Company could hold monthly meetings for realtors and real estate investors on different topics related to title insurance such as "understanding your title policy, how to read your HUD etc.". A realtor could hold monthly meetings for first time home buyers on how to buy a home and get approved for an FHA mortgage. Anyone in any business could hold monthly meetings on the topic related to their business. If the topic is informative and educational, people will come.

If you naturally enjoy public speaking and organizing a meetup group, then it will be easier for you and you'll enjoy yourself more than if you're shy and introverted. If you have a challenge with this, I highly recommend joining your local Toastmasters group. My wife and I both joined the Boca Raton Noon Toastmasters Group. While I no longer attend Toastmasters, being a member is a great way to learn how to make a presentation, give a speech and feel comfortable with public speaking.

I believe when it comes to face to face networking, the most important thing is to love what you do. If you don't love what you do, then how can you take the time every month to teach and explain it to other people? Most people that enjoy what they do would love to talk about it for hours on end. These types of people have no problem running a meetup group. Registering on Meetup.com is free. Once you have registered you can add a picture to your profile and then you can join local groups that are associated with what you are interested in. If you go to, *www.meetup.com*, and type in real estate you will see there are many groups related to real estate in your area. It is also a great way to network with other people who enjoy similar non-work-related hobbies and is a great way to meet new friends.

In order to run a meetup group, you will need to agree to pay $15 per month for at least 3 months. One secret that many organizers on meetup are not aware of is that you can have up to 3 meetup groups per organizer. This means that you could run three different meetup groups using one profile and you would only pay one monthly fee. It is a good idea for you to change the meeting topic monthly in order to keep it interesting for everyone that attends. It is also a good idea to charge a nominal amount from attendees in order to cover or offset some of the cost of the room.

Running your own meetup group will take up some of your time and is a large commitment that requires planning and perseverance. However, it is well worth it as you discover new business and establish friendships along the way. Remember the concept of the "GoGiver" that says people will do business with those people that they know, like and trust. Running a meetup group is the perfect opportunity for them to know you, like you and trust you. As a meeting organizer, you will be providing monthly educational content that your members will learn from and appreciate. Soon they will religiously attend all your meetings and when they do, you will have reached the level of trust where if they are interested in the product that you offer, then they will buy it.

CHAPTER NINETEEN: ADD THIS

*A*dd This is a bookmark and sharing service that allows you to boost traffic back to your web site for free. It does this by making it easier for visitors to share your content. The site can be found at *www.addthis.com*. When you visit the site you simply select your service, select a button style and then get your button. If you want to track how many people click on your button then you can also choose to register and get the analytics. You can place 'Add This' buttons on your website, blog, and almost anywhere online.

By allowing users to share your content, you will increase traffic to your website. Since Google ranks web sites based on how many other websites link back to it, the more links back to your website, the higher you will rank in the search engines. The Add This directory currently has 233 services for sharing and bookmarking including all of the social networking sites that this book talks about. Adding a share this button is very useful for driving relevant traffic back to your website.

In order to drive traffic back to your website, there should be reasons why other readers would click on your article and point it out to others. The only way this will happen is if your article is interesting, useful, or is sharing breaking information that no one knows about. If you don't have anything interesting to write about, then your best bet is to find breaking news about your industry and post it online.

The big challenge will be to write something yourself as opposed to cutting and pasting someone else's thoughts and ideas. The web and blogs in particular are a great medium for you to get your original thoughts into words that others might be able to read and learn from. For example, let's say your blog talks about the current rate of foreclosures in Miami. And say yesterday you went to the court house and the clerk told you that filings were significantly up, and there were a massive amount of cases coming up over the next month. If you had a blog, you might be able to write something about this and give it a provocative headline like: "Massive Amount of Foreclosure Filings Still Coming!" Now if you put together a well thought out article with supporting facts and data, then you could post an article like this on your blog. Make sure that you put your name and your website and company name into the article.

After you have posted your article on your blog make sure to add the "Add This" button above your posting. Once you have done this, start clicking on the share this button and start posting it to every single social networking site. Once you have posted it, other people will see it. And if the title looks good people will click on it. If the article is a good read they will share it with others by clicking on the "Add this" button above the article. If the article is really good, then it can go viral (spread all over the internet).

I have written articles about foreclosures that have been picked up by hundreds of websites and blogs. "Add this" is a large reason why.

CHAPTER TWENTY: EZINEARTICLES

Www.ezinearticles.com, is a great website that allows anyone to write short articles and publish them online. If you are an expert in your field, Ezine articles is a great way to write short, informative articles to share with others. Remember that you should educate and inform others on a topic that you are an expert in. This way, people that are interested in this topic, will be more likely to read it. There are a few other article submission article sites that are worthy of your consideration but Ezine articles is probably the most read and the easiest to use. You can post your articles to these other sites in addition to posting your articles on Ezine Articles.com.

Opening an account with Ezine articles is free and easy. Like with the other social networking sites, add your photo, bio, links to your website and contact information. Try to submit at least 6 articles to Ezine articles with different topics related to your field. You can use the RSS feature on Ezine articles to get your Ezine articles to feed into your website. If you submit a few articles, you will receive "expert author" status which is something useful to put on your blog or website like I have done.

But by far, the most important reason for writing Ezine articles is for search engine optimization (SEO). You see an article relevant to your topic has many key words in it that will be recognized by the search engines. This means that this article is likely to place higher up on the search engine rankings, which in turn will translate into more people reading it. By now you already know that if more people read your article then more people are likely to find your website. And, of course, when they get to your website there will be a capture page to capture their name and email address along with a free product giveaway.

Make sure to write your articles and save them in word format before uploading them to Ezine articles. That way you can also upload the same articles to blogs, other web sites and other article submission websites. These articles will also be good material to use again if someone asks you to write something for their Ezine, blog, magazine or even newspaper article. Make sure that before uploading your articles; include your name and copyright information, so that if someone uses your article on their blog you will get credit. I have thousands of links online from articles that I have written.

After you have written your articles, you can use a company like *http://www.submitinme.com,* to submit your article to literally hundreds of article submission directories. Submitting your articles will distribute your topic and keywords thousands of times all over the internet and will help drive relevant traffic back to your website.

CHAPTER TWENTY ONE:
HOOTSUITE

Since there are so many new social networking sites with more being added daily, it can become quite cumbersome to keep track of all of them. Posting and updating your profiles on so many different sites can be a huge time waster and can take up many hours of each day. For this reason, using a site like *www.hootsuite. com,*can be a huge timesaver. HootSuite allows you to add all of your social networking accounts to your account. For example, you can add Twitter, Facebook, LinkedIn, You Tube, Flickr and your blog to your HootSuite account. You will need to provide your user id and password for each of these social networking sites in order for HootSuite to have access to them. Then you can make one posting and it will show up simultaneously on all of your social networking sites including your blog. This allows you to post simultaneously to multiple social networking sites, will save you a tremendous amount of time and will make your social networking much less tedious.

Remember that the most important thing is to provide valuable content in your field of expertise. For example, my field of expertise is real estate. Every morning, I search the real estate news specifically for topics of interest to Miami real estate investors. If I find something of interest, then I will post a link to it as follows:

1. Find something newsworthy like breaking Miami real estate news to post to HootSuite

2. Go to *www.bit.ly* and use the free URL shortening service to get a short URL link to the story (to fit into the 140-character Twitter limit)

3. Go to HootSuite and log into my account

4. Post comment that is similar to or identical to the headline of the article with a link to the story which will be the bit.ly shortened link. This will be what the user clicks on if they are interested in reading this story.

What is the benefit of doing this? Well first, it will get you in the habit of reading relevant news related to the real estate industry every morning. Second, it will enable you to keep touch with your audience by providing them with valuable and informative content that they might be interested in reading.

The most important benefit is that each one of these posts will create a link on the web which can be crawled by the search engines. For example, assume you belong to twenty online social networking sites. If each of these twenty social networking accounts are added to your HootSuite account, then each time you post a story on HootSuite there will be twenty online links to that story (one for each social networking profile).

If you are in the habit of doing every morning, then each month there will be six hundred new links on the internet that link back to you. If anyone reading any one of those links clicks on your profile then you will have another follower, friend, or visitor to your website.

If you provide a free report linked to a capture page, then there is a good chance you will be able to add a significant portion of this traffic to your database. These are individuals that are interested in your product or service. These individuals may become paying customers at some point in the future. This is a classic example of converting social networking into dollars. The next chapter will talk more specifically about capture pages.

CHAPTER TWENTY TWO: PINTEREST

Pin Your Way to Marketing Perfection

Pinterest allows anybody to create and organize virtual pin boards on almost any topic, then share these pins, which are most commonly images but can also be in video form, to other Pinterest users and across the Internet via websites, blogs, and other social networks. Pins can either be uploaded directly from your computer or mobile device or shared via a website. Since launching in March 2010, Pinterest's popularity has rocketed. When you consider that Pinterest is the second biggest driver of web traffic among social media sites (beaten only by Facebook), it is no surprise that thousands of businesses, including the biggest in the world, already use it as a place to showcase their brand to an audience of over 70 million users, over 75% of whom browse the site on mobiles.

Pinterest users visit the site to search for, browse and collate the things they love and that inspire them. This is where the huge potential for businesses on Pinterest comes into play because plenty of them are shoppers. The most successful pins on Pinterest, whether posted by an individual or a business, all have a couple of things in common: they pair super images with content that solves a problem, inspires a user, offers something desirable or appeals to a hobby or an activity. Think about how these pinnable traits can be applied to your brand as a way for people to discover content about the things they love that have been pinned by you. Think of how to encourage engagement and conversation about your company culture, products, and services and to drive click-through rates to your content outside of Pinterest. For example, a seller of custom

195

dog collars might publish pins about how to teach dog tricks, or how to make home-made dog treats.

While some Pinterest users visit the site with the explicit desire to find a product to purchase, others don't, or are at a different stage of the buying journey. Therefore, the mix of content you provide should appeal to and positively influence both types. In short, if the content you post makes someone want to buy from you, that's great. (Pinterest users often create "wish list boards" as a stepping stone to purchasing products so you'll want to encourage them to add your products to these while browsing). But if it makes them laugh, smile, daydream, or think positively about you, that's a really good sign too. Pins that aren't solely promotional, but lifestyle-based and influential by positive association with your business can be just as effective in the long run; whether your content offers a helpful tip or motivates a user to take an action, that's just more reason for them to repin it to one of their boards for safekeeping and to show off to their followers via their Home screens.

No matter what business you're in, you should use Pinterest to inspire people with words and images. Show them their dreams and aspirations. This means creating boards not only to showcase your products and services, but others that demonstrate interesting and pinnable ideas, themes and concepts that surround it. Even if your brand isn't very visual and you don't think the site would be a good fit, it pays to remember that Pinterest is as much (if not more) about collating and sharing images by others, as pinning your own. For example, a coffee shop may have a board about their drinks and food, but also about the latest trends in coffee culture, such as gadgets, music, interior design, etc. People re-pin and follow accounts on Pinterest because they appeal to their passions and needs, not because they love your latest marketing campaign! Be a resource for pinners and pin with a service mindset, not one obsessed with profit.

Pinterest Profile Optimization

Pinterest's current layout doesn't give a whole lot of scope for customizing the look of your profile, but there are still a few key things you must to do maximize the impact of your account. Sign up as a business or convert your personal Pinterest account.

In November 2012, Pinterest ramped up its support for brands by allowing them to sign up specifically as businesses (instead of just as an individual) and also allowed those brands which already had a Pinterest presence to convert their personal accounts to ones for business. To do either, visit *http://business.pinterest.com*, and select the option that applies to you. Once you're signed up as a business, you'll gain access to a selection of business-specific resources, including Pinterest analytics tools, successful case studies and links to Pinterest buttons and widgets you can place on your website or blog to promote your activity on the site.

Craft an effective username

The first thing you'll want to get right when signing up for Pinterest is your username, which will form the basis of your Pinterest profile's URL (e.g., *www.pinterest.com/yourcompanyname*). You will want to publicize this URL both online and in the real world, so try to keep it short, simple and memorable. The obvious choice is your brand name, but if you have a keyword or slogan related to your company that could work better, especially if your brand's name is longer than the 15-character limit, then consider that instead. In addition, your 'First Name' and 'Last Name' should also reflect your brand, as it will appear prominently at the top of your Pinterest profile. My first and last names could be '500 Social Media' and 'Marketing Tips', for example. If your brand name is short, a last name may not be necessary.

Use the 'About' section to your advantage

The description you write in the 'About' section of Pinterest appears at the top of your profile page and acts to describe your brand and what you do. Crucially, however, it will also appear under your Pinterest URL in Google search results, so make sure to include two or three of your business' most relevant keywords. Don't overdo the length, 160 characters should be plenty. For example, mine reads: "Andrew McCarthy, author of the #1 Amazon Web Marketing

Bestseller, 500 Social Media Marketing Tips. Follow for social media tutorials and infographics!"

Add your website and verify it for trustworthiness

Pretty obvious, this one. Pinterest will display a little 'globe' icon at the top of your profile, which will lead to your website when clicked. It isn't hugely prominent on the Pinterest profile page, but every little bit helps, so don't leave it blank. To show people that you are a trusted source of information, Pinterest allows you to verify your website. Once verified, you'll earn a tick next to its URL on your profile and you'll gain access to Pinterest web analytics. To verify our website on Pinterest, click the "Verify website" button next to the box in which you entered your URL. On the next page, follow the instructions to complete the verification process. You can verify using an HTML file or a Meta tag.

Upload a great profile image

The two most popular types of Pinterest profile images for brands are your company's logo or, if you are the figurehead of your business, a head and shoulders shot, smiling and happy, of course. Pinterest profile images display within a rounded square on your profile page, and within circles next to pinned content and comments. To ensure your logo looks great wherever it appears on the site, upload a square 200 x 200 pixel image, but keep your business logo or face within the central "safe area," away from the corners. Download a template to help you do this (and lots of other great stuff) via the Premium Content Bundle chapter of this book.

Customize the showcase at top of your Pinterest Profile

As a business user, Pinterest allows you to showcase up to five of your most important pin boards in a looping carousel, which sits at the top of your profile. This is the first thing visitors to your Pinterest account see. The perfect way to introduce visitors and show what you offer, such as a collection of your latest products, popular pins from the past, or anything else that fits your business. To start building your brand's showcase, visit your profile on the web and click the edit pencil button in the bottom-right corner of your showcase placeholder, or visit the profile section of account settings. By the way, if you have access to Buyable Pins (Pins that allow people to find and buy your products on Pinterest) setup, your "Shop" will be featured as the first collection in the carousel automatically.

CHAPTER TWENTY THREE: GOOGLE

Get Technical with Google

I am from the tech world; I have been involved in it since the late 90's. In the early days of the internet a small team of programmers led by two aspiring visionaries started a search engine you may have heard of called Google. Now, Google has not only the largest search engine but a ton of business tools you HAVE to take advantage of. As a real estate agent, you need reliable, cheap tools to stay ahead. Google can do this for you.

The first thing you HAVE to do is setup a Gmail account. Gmail is an email account that runs through Google's systems. It has the best anti-spam software; it allows you to check it through a web-based system and can also be pulled using your phone's email system or your computers Outlook or iMail. If you are not familiar with Gmail's interface and want to use your regular email that is also no problem. You can set up the email to forward to that account.

The main reason for this account is to have one login to all of Google's tools. You can now set up different Google tools like analytics, webmaster tools, Google+ account, etc. All of these will help you with your online marketing efforts. I will go into details of each and why you should use them.

Contact Me Quickly with a Google Voice Account

In sports there is a saying "Quickness Wins." This is also very true in business. In the world of real estate if someone is looking at a home and wants to look at it they are going to contact someone. If they are not able to get that person it is highly unlikely that they will wait around. In order to make sure you always get that call I recommend a Google Voice number. A Google voice number will allow you to ring your home, office, and cell phone every time you receive a call to your number. It also transcribes voice mails into e-mails and text messages. This is very important when you need to get back in touch with leads in a very short time frame in the highly competitive world real estate.

Make sure this is the number you put on all of your materials. That way you can always get every call. Do not worry about getting crazy calls in the middle of the night (unless you want crazy calls in the middle of the night) because you can turn the calls to voicemail during off business hours or set a schedule for the number to follow. During the day you will get calls to your cell, office and then your home. In the afternoon you could set it to go to your cell and home, and at night to go to voicemail, which you could get in the form of a text. This is a number you will be able to keep and use on all your advertising for years to come, no matter which office you are with or what cell phone company.

Webmaster Tools

Setting up a Google webmaster tools account will allow you to get Google's take on your website, see how it goes and diagnose any problems that could impact your ranking on Google. It tells you search queries that were used to reach your site. It shows who is linking back to your site. This is very important because Google gives extra importance to sites that have a lot of other websites linking back to them. It will let you know if there are any errors on any page of your website and how your site performs speed wise.

Google Analytics

This is a great tool for tracking visitors and time onsite. It is the best for seeing where your visitors have come from, what pages they visited and what pages they left on. Another great feature is the map feature. You can zero in on where the traffic is coming from the city and state that you are getting visits from. This is great for real estate agents who get leads from specific areas; they can then use this data to market in those areas on say, a small Google ads campaign.

Google Alerts

Setting up Google alerts is something you need to do. There are plenty of reasons to setup alerts. The main reason is that you are your own brand online. You have to police your reputation online as no one else who will do this for you. Using Google Alerts allows you to get an alert every time a new instance of a particular keyword comes up in Google. If you set up an alert, for the keyword "New Home in Hoboken" someone writes a blog about how they are looking for a "new home in Hoboken", you will get an email from Google with a link to this blog. Hand delivered information to your email box from Google. You can setup as many alerts as possible and turn them on and off as you want. This way if you are getting alerts that mean nothing or "Spam Alerts" as some call them, it is easy to stop getting them.

The main thing is that you set up an alert for your name. This way you can monitor your brand online. If someone says something about you, then you will know about it before most will ever find it. Remember it is up to you to police your reputation online.

Google Places & Local

Google places are sometimes called Google Local. It is the place where you list your business. If you have ever searched for a web design agency and there are a few of the local agencies in a list above the results, then you have seen the results of business listings. These are above the search listings and offer a great way for you to get your business out there to potential clients. According to Google, over one-third of people looking for real estate information on Google are searching for agents or brokers. You can also submit multiple locations with a data file and conveniently manage and control listings. You can list your home office, your firm desk, etc. can be listed in Google local and give you additional exposure.

Google Map

You can post your listings by submitting them to Google. By providing your real estate listings to them, it will broaden your distribution and receive free traffic and leads through natural search results on Google properties. Real estate search results will be displayed on Google Maps, allowing users to immediately zero in on the neighborhoods most attractive to them. This will show your available property when users are searching, placing your home in front of someone when they are ready to buy, puts you in a prime position. This also allows people to use Google maps to map their drive, get directions and find out what other places are close by. They can see where the closest grocery store is, map the distance to their work etc.

Create a YouTube Channel

I will tell you in this book to take video. Talk about yourself, talk about the houses, talk about your clients, talk about the area. The main thing is that you are talking and getting your information out to people looking for new home information. Positioning yourself as an expert is key to gaining the trust of the visitors to your YouTube channel. If it is a home walkthrough, a simple update about the local housing market or a tip to clients you should be using video. Google says that over 90% of American homebuyers look for videos when searching for a home. Give them what they want.

The main thing that people do not realize about YouTube is that it is a community. When you are looking at videos on YouTube, the next time check out the comments at the bottom. You will notice that there are references to other users, videos and information that will illustrate that people use the website not only as a place to find great videos but also to interact with others. With the introduction of Google+ you will see an increase in the chatter and social aspect of You Tube. Take full advantage of this.

Google+ profile

Setting up a Google profile is probably one of the things you HAVE to do. The main reason is that it will help to brand yourself and even if you do not care to use internet marketing to brand yourself, you have to use social media. If you plan on using both, then Google+ is a network you have to be a part of. Google+ has all the perks of the older social networks like Facebook and twitter, with one district difference. The ability to choose who sees your status updates. This way you can keep your business updates out of your personal streams and your personal "I got so hammered last night", updates off your business streams.

There is also the key fact that Google owns this social network. Everything you share on this network will be tied to you and your personal brand. Links to relevant real estate articles, information on mortgage rates, foreclosure information, etc. Google reads all this to get a bead on who you are as a person, what kind of "brand" you are. Use this page to display your business side but do not lose the personal touches that make social networking the best way to market you.

CHAPTER TWENTY FOUR: CAPTURE PAGES

Capture pages are also known as squeeze pages or landing pages. They are called these various names because the purpose of these pages is to get internet surfers to land on them and then "capture" their information. For example, in the previous chapter, I mentioned posting a link to a real estate news story via HootSuite to various social networking sites. As an example, imagine that your tag line in your profile on your social networking site said something like "Free Report: Top Ten Ways To Buy Real Estate Using Other People's Money". Now imagine if one of those readers of that news story clicked on the link to see the free report. When they clicked on the link they would be transported to a landing page or capture page.

The capture page has only one purpose. The purpose of the capture page is to capture their first name and email address. Of secondary importance are the persons' last name, telephone number and mailing address. Many capture pages only ask for the first name and email address. Since most online marketing campaigns are now via email the email address is the most important information to capture.

Ideally, a capture page should look like the image below, with the sole purpose of getting your prospects details to lead them further into the sales funnel.

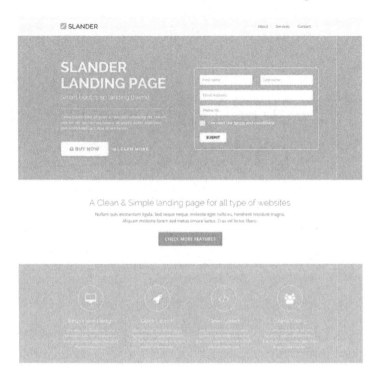

Random internet surfers will not simply give you their name and email address. You will need to offer them something of value like a free report which they will get if they enter their name and email address. If the information is valuable to them then they will put in their name and email address in order to get that report. A very small percentage will lie and use a fake email address. For an example of how a capture page works please visit one of the capture pages that I created at this link: *http://www.cheaphousesinsouthflorida.com*

Users that click on the above capture page are offered a free eBook in adobe acrobat (pdf) format. All they have to do to get the eBook is put in their name and email address and they get a copy of their free eBook sent to them via email. In exchange for that, I get their name and email address and I get to add them to my database. From that point forward, whenever I send an email to my database they will also get this email.

If they would like to stop receiving these emails all they need to do is click on the "unsubscribe" link at the bottom of any email and they will be permanently deleted from my database. Less than 20% of subscribers unsubscribe from the database. Most subscribers stay there and keep receiving the emails. And you know why? Because they are interested in the subject matter! Then when I send out my wholesale deal blast one of these people might buy a house from me.

One month later when I send out an invitation to attend a local real estate investment club meeting, some of these subscribers might attend the meeting (if they are local). Once they are at this meeting they might decide they are interested in one of my products, such as an upcoming Distressed Real Estate Boot Camp. If they sign up for one of my products whether it is by purchasing a book, Home Study Course or Boot Camp then I have just converted internet traffic from a landing page into sales revenue. I do this every single day. And I do it quite effectively. You can do this too. It is not difficult at all. It does take some time and effort to setup, but the best part is that once it is set up it runs forever. It runs 24 hours a day, 365 days a year. And it runs all over the world.

To get started, all you need to do is write a report or something of value that you can give away for free. Then create a capture page and set up an auto responder which will send them an automated email and save their information into your database. You will use this auto responder to send them emails in the future. We show people how to do this at our Real Estate Internet Marketing Boot Camp. For more information about this boot camp please visit *http://www. realestatemarketingbootcamp.com.*

Chapter Twenty Four: Capture Pages

As I have mentioned previously throughout this book, the best way to get internet traffic is to do it for free. And the best and cheapest way to do this is through internet marketing methods utilizing capture pages and using social networking sites like Facebook, Twitter, YouTube and LinkedIn. The expensive way to get traffic is to use Google AdWords and pay for a payperclick campaign. I do both. Both are effective. If you can afford to incorporate a Pay per Click campaign, then I encourage you to do so. But first make sure your landing pages and conversions work before you start spending money. Use free social networking sites to test the landing pages and conversions.

You can utilize a capture page very effectively with a pay per click campaign. With this type of campaign, you are paying for certain key words that a user might enter into a search engine like Google. When they enter these keywords, your ad will display depending on how much you bid for that keyword relative to other companies that are bidding on that same keyword. Google pay per click campaigns are very effective but can get quite expensive as you add keywords. Most SEO companies recommend that you have no more than 10 keywords and that your keywords are related directly to the keywords on your capture page. If a user types in one of your keywords into Google, then they might click on your link and end up on your landing page. This will then give you an opportunity to capture their information. You can find out more information about Google's Ad words pay per click service and how it works at: *www. adwords.google.com.*

Another related and relevant topic for you to explore further is search engine optimization (SEO). This concept is a way of having relevant content (written text) on your website or capture page on your site that will drive users to your capture page without having to pay for a pay per click campaign. Usually you are better off hiring a professional SEO company than you are trying to figure out how to do it yourself.

However, it can become quite costly to begin employing pay per click campaigns in order to get traffic for a free product. Payperclick campaign soften work better when you can immediately convert someone into a paying customer. For example, if you have a product that they could potentially click on and buy immediately. However, this is not always the case. In some businesses, like real estate, the value of a lead can be quite high. For example, there are real estate companies that will pay as much as $50 for a valuable lead (someone that enters their name and email address into a capture page).

How much you spend driving traffic to your website relative to how much money you make out of that traffic is called conversion. For example, if I spend $1 per click to bring people to my landing page and one out of every five people signs up by putting in their name and email address then it will cost me $5 per lead to add them to my database.

If my objective is to sell them a $1,000 boot camp, then I would need to sell at least one out of every twenty people in my database or the campaign will not be effective. Considering that most online campaigns have closing ratios of less than 1%, it would be very difficult to employ this type of marketing continuously for most small businesses. However, some businesses use pay per click campaigns very effectively and swear by them. If you are interested in learning more about pay per click I suggest you read "The Ultimate Guide to Google AdWords" by Perry Marshall.

If you are using social networking as a driver of traffic to your landing page then this effectively means that the traffic is free. Since the traffic is free it does not matter how many people sign up or what the percentage of conversion is. Either way a free potential customer is better than no customer. Fine tuning and tweaking the information on the capture page and the free content is usually a much better option for most small business than a pay per click campaign. It is much cheaper to pay a web designer $100 to make some changes to a capture page than it is to spend $50 every day on Google AdWords.

The reason is because overtime the cost of the payperclick campaign will really add up. Since the capture page is not costing you money, you can experiment with different wording, different designs and see which works best. It is very useful to make note of competitor's capture pages and to see which ones' appeal to you as a consumer. The better your message and the better your free content the more likely you are to be able to capture their information. If you can capture their information for free then you can add another customer to your database. Designing a decent professional looking capture page should cost you no more than $250.

CHAPTER TWENTY FIVE: EMAIL ADDRESSES

This part is so basic but yet so important that I felt it necessary to include it in this book as a chapter. Every time that I go to a networking event, I receive many business cards. Whenever I look through these business cards I am amazed at how many people make this mistake. Hopefully after reading this chapter you will not be one of them. If you are in business then you should not have a business email address that ends in gmail.com, yahoo.com, hotmail.com, aol.com, bellsouth.net, Comcast.net, etc. These email addresses are your private email address where you receive email. They are **not** what you should have on your business card. Your business card and website should have an email address that says your *name@yourdomainname.com*.

Your personal email address should remain personal. The only one that should know your personal email address is you. The only time you should use your personal email to configure your mail servers in Outlook or on your iPad or iPhone, or whatever email server client you use. These settings are easy to configure in a program like Microsoft Outlook, Gmail, Yahoo or whatever email server you use.

You can set up incoming mail to be forwarded from your hosting domain to your personal email address. Configuring your email this way has many advantages. First, you can make your email account with your hosting company a "catch all" account. This means that it will catch all emails including those where the email address is not typed correctly.

The second advantage is that if you had more than one business you could separate them. For example, if you had a hobby business on the side, you could establish a domain name for that business and an email address for that business. Many people have multiple businesses and find this quite useful.

It is extremely unprofessional to have an email address like *jsmith123@hotmail.com*. Many people do not know that this is unprofessional. If you are going to do that at least use Gmail so people will know you are cool. If your company has a website, then your email address should be affiliated with your web domain name. If your company does not have a website, then you should ask yourself why not? The World Wide Web has been around since 1993.That was 25 years ago! Where have you been for all this time? If you have a business, then you need to have a website. And if you have a website, you can have a custom email address related to your domain name.

Please remember that your email address should match your domain. There are absolutely no exceptions to this ever. A domain costs $6 per month to host and includes multiple free email addresses. Visit *http://www.godaddy.com,* for registering a domain name and a hosting account for your website and email address. Another good reason why you want to have your own domain name is because you want to control your spam. For example, services like AOL have spam filters which are in place to block spam. This is great if they are blocking emails that you don't want to get. However, if you are signing up for your competitor's capture pages to see how they operate, then it is not so great when you don't get all of your emails.

Anyone that bulk emails (sends out emails to a large amount of email addresses) is going to get their emails stopped by a spam filter. Many companies now email their clients in bulk which means that if you use services like AOL you are going to be missing a lot of emails. There is no logical valid reason to use a service like AOL. &You should get a free Google Gmail address if you don't already have an email address from your high-speed internet service provider. Then, when you establish your domain and your email to go with your domain simply have all your emails forwarded to your Gmail email account.

Chapter Twenty Five: Email addresses

It is a good idea to try and stick with one company name or username for multiple sites. The same concept applies to email addresses. If your company name is *www.wholesalerealestateforum.com,* then you should try to get matching email addresses that correspond to these names, even if you never intend to ever use them. For example:

- wholesalerealestateforum@gmail.com
- wholesalerealestateforum@yahoo.com

This way you can protect your name and prevent someone else from getting your branded name as an email address. If you ever decide at a later stage to set up a Flickr account, which requires a Yahoo User Id you will already have one with a name that matches your business. Then on your profile page, your bio, photo and description on Yahoo will all match your website name, brand name, etc. This is important because Yahoo is just one more example of a social networking site that you can use. Your email address has to end in Yahoo.com but it can start with anything. You might as well make it match your company name. This will be hard to do if someone already has the name. That is why I recommend reserving the email addresses so that no one else can take them on all the major sites.

The same concept applies with YouTube where you need a Google Gmail address. At a bare minimum, register your custom domain, a Gmail email address and a Yahoo email address with the same user id.

CHAPTER TWENTY SIX: ONLINE AND OFFLINE NETWORKS

Please note that the more social networking sites you belong to, the more likely it will be for you and your business to be noticed and seen by others. Also keep in mind, if you belong to social networking sites, take the time to update your profile. You should at least have a photo, an email address, a contact phone number, a website link back to your website and a short bio about yourself. Social networking is very much a medium where you get what you put into it.

If you post a profile online and never log in or do anything with it, you are wasting time. Plan to allocate at least 30 minutes each day to social marketing. Login to your sites, share your message, log off and go about your day. If you do every day, people will find you and you will begin to be well known in your industry. HootSuite can really be a big time saver for achieving this as quickly as possible.

Add some old-fashioned face to face marketing to your social networking and over time you will be a person that is well known in your industry. Remember, people do business with those people that they know, like, and trust. They have to first know you and social marketing is one of the best ways for them to first find out about you. Then they have to like you, which they cannot do unless they have some face to face interaction with you. Meetups and networking events are a great way to get face to face interaction with these people. And finally, they have to trust you, so you need to establish yourself as an expert in your field. You need to be someone that knows their profession well. It will be hard to do this if you don't like what you do for a living. Love what you do and do it with passion. Or find something else to do.

You also need to be a person of good character that is honest and well-spoken of by others. Remember the four key words of what I call the "CHIP Principle". Be consistent, be honest, act with integrity and above all be persistent. I am constantly amazed at how people constantly change their business brand or idea or openly have hostile dishonest interactions with other people in their industry. Then they come to the networking events and wonder why business is slow. I always point out the CHIP Principle to these people. Most of them do not know that other people are saying bad things about them. Remember this. If you act dishonestly or unethically in your business transactions, more people will hear about it than if you act honestly and ethically. People assume you will be honest and ethical. If you are not they will make sure everyone else knows about it. And that is bad for business and all the networking in the world can't help you solve that problem.

If people know what you do, respect you, like you and know that you are good at what you do, then why would they not utilize your services? There can be only three reasons.

Reason number one is that your product or service is too expensive (or someone is able to do it for less).

Reason number two is that your product or service is not needed or wanted by the general public.

Reason number three is that you are not perceived as an expert in what you do. This is the most likely reason for people not utilizing your service. You can solve this by:

Networking online and offline.

If you are sure that your pricing is good and that your product is something that people need and want, then you should ask yourself honestly if you really know everything that there is to know in your field. One good way to find out is to network with other professionals. Ask yourself if any of them know more than you do about your industry. If the answer is yes, then strive to learn more, be better, and become an expert.

CHAPTER TWENTY SEVEN: YOUR PERSONAL REFERRAL TEAM

One of the key concepts that I learned from the book the "Go Giver" by Bob Burg and John David Mann was the concept of your own personal referral team. You should have your own personal referral team, which is like your board of directors. These people are business affiliates that you do business with. You should be promoting their business and they should be promoting yours.

Becoming a member of a real estate company will help you choose and find your personal referral team. You will not like everyone that you network with, and everyone that you network with will not necessarily like you. Also, some individuals will be easier to refer business to than others. However, over time you will develop a personal referral network of business professionals.

For example, I am in the business of real estate. I use the professional services of title companies, appraisers, inspectors, mortgage brokers, realtors, handymen, general contractors, architects, etc.

Many people ask me to refer quality people to them and I always do. In turn, these people refer new clients to me that might be interested in learning how to invest in real estate. The key concept is that you know these people well enough to know that they know what they are doing. You also have to be comfortable referring them business and knowing they will take care of your clients and not make you look bad. Referrals can make you look good or they can make you look bad. It is very important to make sure that you treat other people's referrals in a timely and professional manner.

If you already have people that you do business with on a daily business, then you should be referring business to them. If they are good at what they do, then you should make a point of referring their business. In time, you will find that people will refer business back to you. After a year or two, you will develop some key relationships with individuals that you do a lot of business with. These individuals should become your personal referral network and be a part of your team to help promote you and your business.

In turn, you should be their personal referral network and should help promote them and their business. Naturally you want to make sure that you are working with people that you know, like and trust. You want to make sure that these people are ethical, know what they are doing in their industry and will always act with the highest integrity. Your personal referral network should be willing to give positive testimonials about you to others. These testimonials should also be used on your website, promotional material, videos, capture pages, YouTube, etc.

Remember, if you only say good things about yourself, then you are just a self-promoter. If other people say good things about you, then it is perceived to be true. Make sure that you align yourself with the right people and distance yourself from people that could harm your reputation or your business images.

CHAPTER TWENTY EIGHT:
BUILDING YOUR EMAIL LIST

Regardless of what type of product you are selling, you will need to have a database of customers and potential customers. The easiest and cheapest way to market to this database is via an email campaign. The easiest and cheapest way to get new customers into your database is via a capture page. There are many database companies out there, but I am going to specifically talk to you about only one of them. *www.1shoppingcart.com,* is by far the most popular program for adding customers to an online database. They also offer the added benefit of allowing you to upgrade your account to provide merchant services (credit cards) and shopping cart capability for Instant online checkout.

I am talking specifically about the autoresponder service of 1shoppingcart, which as of this writing, is only $35 per month.

Subscribing to the auto responder, allows you to create customized messages and capture "forms" for your capture pages. The great thing about 1shoppingcart is that you can add unlimited auto responders and up to 10,000 email addresses for the same monthly rate of only $35 per month.

Email may not seem like a popular form of digital communication, but it still represents one of the most efficient forms of marketing. Email is universal, with over 3.7 billion email users around the world, hence you are guaranteed to attract prospects through this channel. Furthermore, email marketing has one of the highest ROIs of any digital marketing process, with an average dollar spent bringing in a return of $44.

To begin, you need to collate your email list and seek permission from your prospects. After doing this, create the email content, which should typically include newsletters, product updates, promotions, links to blog posts, videos, and more.

nce you have successfully created the content, the next step is to categorize your email list based on factors like purchasing history, demographics, and buyer journey stage (more on this later), and to create personalized, targeted emails based on those factors. You will also need to decide the frequency with which you want to send emails to the prospects.

While some prospects might be a fan of daily updates, others will respond better to periodic reminders.

When you have a web designer create your capture page, you will need to give them the form code received from 1 shopping cart. Each auto responder has a unique number, which is the auto responder id. This allows 1 shopping cart to know which customer account is associated with the auto responder message and also which message to associate with it. You can simply copy and paste the code into your email, send it to your web designer and they should be able to handle it for you.

Usually the only information that you need in the form for your capture page is name, email address, and telephone number. I always make the name and email address compulsory, but the telephone number is voluntary. This means that as long as they provide me with their name and email address, they will get their free report. Their name and email address will then automatically be added to my 1 shopping cart database. Going forward all emails that I send to my database will automatically go to them as well. As I mentioned previously, if they want to unsubscribe from these emails they simply need to click on unsubscribe and they will automatically be removed from the database.

It is imperative to have an online database like this that continues to grow daily. Strive to have five to ten names per day being added to your database. Over time, your database will become a powerhouse. I currently have tens of thousands of names in my database. When I send an email about a house for sale, it goes to tens of thousands of people. If only 1% are interested, that translates into a lot of potential buyers. This is why most of my wholesale houses sell in less than 48 hours.

The more capture pages you have, the more people will be added to your database. Internet marketers refer to your database of names and email addresses as "your list". The bigger your list, the more you can sell and the more money you can make. If you have a big enough list, then you can make thousands of dollars every time you send an email. Strive to educate, add value and provide valuable information in your free reports and you will have no problem adding many people to your database. Finally, please remember that it takes time to build a list. If you are adding five names a day to a database, it will take you an entire year to have less than two thousand names in your database. Imagine what you could do with two thousand potential customers and start working on your capture page and your online database today.

I speak to many people that tell me that they don't have anything to say of any value (for their free product). I spoke to one lady that was a real estate appraiser. These are some of the ideas that I gave her: Create a free report about what factors influence your appraisal the most. Offer a free report about what renovations homeowners can do that would add the most value to their house. The same individual asked me what they could possibly say in an email. I offered how about "Special for this month only 20% off all appraisals".

Everyone has something to sell and everyone has something to say. You have information about your area of expertise inside your head that other people would like to know. Take some time to think creatively about your product or service or message and you will come up with something great.

CHAPTER TWENTY NINE: SEARCH ENGINE OPTIMIZATION (SEO)

Before we explore Search Engine Optimization (SEO), we must first understand paid search engine advertising. Search engine advertising is a type of marketing whereby websites can pay a fee in exchange for having their website appear at the top of search results when internet users type particular key words into a search engine; this type of marketing is also referred to as sponsored search advertisements. This method of advertising is advantageous to businesses because it keeps their website from being buried in the search results.

In the same way that businesses can take on their own social media marketing (rather than using paid social media advertisings), Search Engine Optimization offers marketing professionals a way to increase their visibility in a search engine's results without having to pay for Search Engine Advertising. SEO as an advertising approach capitalizes on the search engines algorithm for returning search results. In a way, SEO outsmarts the search engine by including key words that will drive visibility of websites in unpaid search results.

SEO as a Digital Marketing Tool

Search Engine Optimization (SEO) plays an integral part in digital marketing because it entails boasting your website ranking and ensuring that the site is exposed enough to attract consumer traffic.

For instance, if you owned an independent cell phone e-commerce store that competes with a brand like Samsung, then SEO is the best way to make sure that when a prospect searches for phones for sale, your website will be visible on the first search engine result page.

SEO is split into two categories: on-page and off-page.

On-page SEO deals with the technical optimization processes you want to run on your own website, and it involves actions like creating and optimizing engaging content, improving site speed, optimizing page elements with keywords, using the right URL structure, creating internal links, king title tags, and dividing content using headings.

Off-page SEO focuses solely on creating a strong chain of backlinks to your site because this proves to death engines that your site is valuable, authoritative and relevant, which is essential for higher rankings.

CHAPTER THIRTY: ENGAGING FRIENDS, FOLLOWERS & FANS

While each social media network operates in a slightly different way and uses individual terms for people with whom you are linked, the key to driving visibility to your product or brand remains the same: attract "Friends", "Followers", "Fans", "Connections" or whatever they are called in the particular network you are using.

While we have briefly covered a variety of useful tactics for expanding your visibility to customers and potential buyers under each social media marketing section, the approach to exposing your brand to your target audience will remain the same regardless of the network you chose to utilize. The best way to involve your network is to keep it simple, generate excitement and create opportunities for engagement. For Twitter or Instagram, use hashtags to control messaging related to your brand. These hashtags can be tied to a special event, seasonal promotions or sales. Encourage people to use the hashtags by placing signage wherever your product is sold (including your website).

Make sure your customers are aware of your specific Twitter account. Make it easy for customers to sing your praises by telling them how to find you on Twitter. Don't forget to include your Twitter handle, as you may be hard to find among the other 300 million users. Use signage wherever your brand is represented, including your website.

Encourage people to get excited and involved with your product or brand. Be creative and provide opportunities for consumers to have fun. This can be accomplished in many ways including setting up an area where your customers have props and encourage them to take selfies that they can share on their network (and yours!). Ultimately, your key to success will rely on the quality of your network. Building cheerleaders for your product is easy once you have established your base of supporters. This will eventually be the group to whom you promote your product or brand. This overarching strategy is effective regardless of whether you're tweeting, posting on Facebook, or pinning information on Pinterest.

CHAPTER THIRTY ONE: CONVERTING FRIENDS, FOLLOWERS AND FANS INTO CUSTOMERS

Consumers love to hear about new products and services from people they know and trust. In fact, people are more likely to try a product if it is recommended by a friend rather than seen in an advertisement. Social networking offers people a platform on which to share their opinions on a variety of topics, including products and service recommendations. We've already covered ways to make people excited about your brand, now it's time to turn your network into sales revenue.

Offering your social network unique and exclusive buying opportunities will drive consumer sales, as customers won't want to miss out on their chance to participate. Encourage sales by creating limited product opportunities that are only available to a select group. Alternately, host an exclusive, invite-only event for your social media followers. Once you've rewarded your social media network with special offers, don't waste their positive feedback. Encourage your customers to share their positive experience on social media. Create a special place where you can feature individuals who have praised your brand, but be sure to get their permission. Most importantly, make it easy for those in your network to buy your product. Exposing people to your promotional post is great, but it won't result in a sale if it lacks a link to your website.

CONCLUSION

I hope that you have learned something that will benefit you from reading this book. I would really like to see you succeed as an internet marketer and see you become better at promoting yourself and your business, both online and offline. If you utilize the material in this book, you will notice a significant improvement in how many people know you and your business. You will rapidly increase your network of friends and over time this will translate into additional revenue. But you must be patient. It takes time to develop real relationships. If you are a real estate investor, agent, or wholesaler, then you will be able to use much of the material in this book to really help you ramp up your business as a real estate investor.

I wish you the best of success in your internet marketing, social networking and real estate investing. I hope to see you at one of our real estate events soon. Remember, this is the best time in your lifetime to get started as a real estate investor. Overcome your fears and start taking action TODAY.

Printed in Great Britain
by Amazon